The Psychology of Spas and Wellbeing

The spa industry has a rich history and culture of holistic healing, but has only recently begun to seek a more scientific foundation for its offerings. Meanwhile, modern medicine and healthcare are borrowing from what spas have successfully applied for centuries to better recognize the holistic nature of human wellbeing. This guide provides you, the spa or wellness professional, with the latest scientific research in wellbeing to assess the evidence of the spa industry's impact on health and to explore applications and interventions that could be used to create a new, more effective healing institution that combines the best of science and philosophy.

D1419820

The Psychology of Spas and Wellbeing

A Guide to the Science of Holistic Healing

Jeremy McCarthy

Picture a dangerous cliff where people are continually falling off and getting hurt. Ambulances come to pick up the injured and take them to the hospital, where high costs are needed to bring them back to health. Now think about how much smarter it would be for someone to build a fence at the top of that cliff – a fence that would prevent people from falling off in the first place. Spas are fences.

Alex Szekely

Contents

Contents vii

Preface xi

Introduction 2

1 The World of Spas 4
   The History of Spa 4
      Principles of Spa 4
      Spas and Alternative Medicine 5
      Health by Water 6
      The Historic Ubiquitousness and Popularity of Spas 8
   The Spa Industry Today 9
      Pampering and Luxury or Wellness and Essential Self Care? ... 10
      Pampering as a Part of Wellness 11
   The Role of Spas in Society 12
      The Role of Society in Health Care 13
      Spas and Positive Health 14
      Spas and Positive Aging 15

2 Mind, Body, and Spirit in the Spa 18
   Holistic Healing and the Domains of Spa 18
      The Philosophy of Mind-Body Healing 19
      The Emotional Connection between Mind and Body 20
      The Role of the Mind in Holistic Healing 21
   Physical Fitness and Exercise 22
      Somaesthetics 23
      Inner and Outer Dimensions of Holistic Wellbeing 24
      Psychological Benefits of Exercise 25
   Spirituality in Spas 27
      Spirit as Emotion 27
      Spirit as Energy 28
      Spirit as Soul 28

3 Spas and the Psychology of Wellbeing 30
   Psychology of Spa 30
      The Physical Benefits of Spa 30
      The Science of Spa 31

The Psychological Impact of Spa 33
The Effect of Person...34
The Power of Touch...36
Energy Work..39
The Power of the Mind in Healing.......................................41
Intention and the Placebo Effect 41
The Role of the Mind in Healing.......................................43
Mechanisms of the Placebo Effect.....................................44
The Mind's Impact on Health 46
The Effect of Time and Mindfulness 47

4 Positive Psychology and Spas 49
Positive Psychology, The Science of Flourishing 49
The Birth of a New Branch of Psychology....................51
Positive Psychology Is Based on Empirical Research 52
Applied Positive Psychology 53
The How of Happiness 54
Spas and the Good Life 55
Spas and a Life of Pleasure 55
Comforts and Pleasures in the Spa World......................56
Types of Pleasure in the Spa...57
Going beyond Pleasure 58
The Intrinsic Nature of Spa..59
Pleasure, Engagement, and Meaning: The Full Life 60
From Happiness to Flourishing 61
Application of Positive Psychology in Spas..........................62
The Power of Positive Questions 63
Positive Questions and Spa Guest Experience................65
Peak-end Theory 66
Paradox of Choice 67
Gratitude 69

5 Spas and Stress...71
A Primer on Stress 71
The Good Side of Stress 72
Stress and the Mind 73
The Science of Stress 74
When Good Stress Goes Bad 76
Spas and Stress Relief..77
Spa Treatments for Stress Relief.......................................77
The Relaxation Response in the Spa Setting....................79

Mind-body Exercises 80
Fitness and Exercise... 82
Stress and Nutrition... 83
Happiness and Stress.. 84
Pampering versus Wellness... 84

6   **The Spa Lifestyle** 86
The Science of Changing Behavior 87
    The Psychology of Behavior Change............................... 87
    The Stages of Change 88
    Self-Determination Theory 90
    Motivational Interviewing.. 91
    Mindfulness and Self-Compassion.................................. 92
Developing Willpower... 93
    Self-regulation 93
    Mindset... 97
    Self-efficacy 99
Goal Theory 100
    Goal Setting and Behavior Change................................100
    Wanting What You Want to Want....................................101
    Writing Goals Down..102
    Hope Theory 103
    Perseverance and "Grit" 103
    Implementation Intentions 104
Habits 107
Rituals and Daily Practices..108
Beyond the Spa...110

7   **Measuring a Spa's Impact on Wellbeing** 111
Subjective Wellbeing in the Spa...111
    Measuring Subjective Wellbeing.....................................112
    Challenges of Measuring Subjective Wellbeing in the Spa 113
    Business Impact of Measuring Wellbeing 115

8   **Conclusion** 117

References..121

Preface

This guide for the spa and wellness professional is the culmination of years of research in the field of positive psychology combined with a lifelong career of opening and operating luxury resort spas. I started my hotel career over twenty years ago as a lifeguard at the Four Seasons Biltmore Resort while studying psychology at the University of California at Santa Barbara.

Unfortunately, psychology at the time was profoundly negative — concerned only with the things that go wrong with people. But I focused my studies on the areas that interested me most: human behavior, motivation, performance, and happiness, and directly applied them throughout my hospitality career in ways that helped me to serve and lead others.

As my professional responsibilities evolved specifically into resort spas, the application of psychology became even more important to my work. While most spas marketed themselves around the scope and magnificence of their facilities, the quality and ingredients of their products, and the skills and techniques of their therapists, I realized that the real impact of a spa happened on the psychological level, in other words, how we make a person *feel*. I developed my career focusing on the science and *psychology* of the spa experience from the standpoints of facility design, product and treatment development, customer service, employee development, and leadership.

After decades of developing my own applications and treatments to create optimal spa experiences, I learned about the developing (and now increasingly popular) field of positive psychology, focused on optimal human functioning. I enrolled in the Master of Applied Positive Psychology program at University of Pennsylvania, spearheaded by Marty Seligman, the founder of positive psychology and author of *Learned Optimism*, *Authentic Happiness* and *Flourish*.

When I graduated in 2009 with my MAPP degree, I continued my studies by launching "The Psychology of Wellbeing" (http://psychologyofwellbeing.com), a blog dedicated to my investigations into the subject of holistic wellness, continuing my research and writing on wellbeing with the same academic fervor that was required of the MAPP program. I publish a new, researched article on the blog each week covering all aspects of holistic wellbeing.

I am excited to share with you what I have learned from my studies. The spa industry has a rich history and culture of holistic healing, but has only recently begun to seek a more scientific foundation for its offerings. Meanwhile, modern medicine and healthcare are borrowing from what spas have successfully applied for centuries to better recognize the holistic nature of human wellbeing. This guide provides you, the spa or wellness professional, with the latest scientific research in wellbeing to assess the evidence of the spa industry's impact on health and to explore applications and interventions that could be used to create a new, more effective healing institution that combines the best of science and philosophy.

I hope the compilation of research in the following pages opens your eyes (as it has mine) to the infinite possibilities for human wellbeing and the enormous contribution that the world of spas can bring to humanity.

P.S. I'd love to hear your thoughts about the ideas contained within this guide. Feel free to write to me at jeremy@psychologyofwellbeing.com.

Acknowledgments

Through my university studies, and the development of my blog, I have learned from the top experts in the fields of human health and happiness: Mihalyi Csikszentmihalyi (flow and engagement [his book *Flow: The Psychology of Optimal Experience* was my first introduction to positive psychology and probably the book that has changed my life more than any other]), Ray Fowler (psychological benefits of fitness and exercise [Ray served as the advisor for my thesis capstone on "The Psychology of Spas and Wellbeing," which served as the foundation for this text]), Brent Bauer (complementary medicine [Brent served as the medical advisor to the International Spa Association for which I served on the board of directors for several years]), Chris Peterson (strengths, relationships), Roy Baumeister (self-regulation and willpower), Angela Duckworth (perseverance), Barbara Fredrickson (positive emotions), Todd Kashdan (mindfulness), Ed Diener (health and happiness), Ira Prilleltensky (wellbeing), Barry Schwartz (the paradox of choice), George Vaillant (emotion and spirituality), Karen Reivich (resilience), Kenneth Pargament (spirituality) and of course Marty Seligman and James Pawelski, the directors of University of Pennsylvania's Center for Positive Psychology. There are many more who are cited in the pages that follow. I am grateful to them all.

The Psychology of
Spas and Wellbeing

A Guide to the Science of Holistic Healing

Introduction

For thousands of years, across borders and across cultures, societies have had some version of a "spa," each of which has offered the promise of delivering an improvement to health and/or quality of life. At times, they have been more medicinal for the purposes of curing disease and enhancing health. At other times, they have been more recreational, a place to go to relax, socialize and have pleasurable experiences. Today, spas continue to exhibit a dual identity as retreats for healing, and also as getaways for luxurious pampering and pleasure.

The International Spa Association (ISPA) has defined spas in the following way: "Spas are places devoted to enhancing overall wellbeing through a variety of professional services that encourage the renewal of mind, body and spirit" (ISPA, 2006c). The fact that spas have been a popular activity across cultures for so much of recorded history gives some validity to the benefits of visiting a spa. But how, specifically, do spas encourage "renewal of mind, body and spirit"? It is easy to immediately identify the benefits to the body by looking at some of the therapeutic offerings from the spa realm. Spas typically offer a range of massage, skincare, and heat and water therapies that are designed to improve circulation, detoxify the tissues, and facilitate healing. But how does a spa impact the mind and the spirit? What is the psychological impact of a spa?

Is it that the body is renewed through therapeutic physical treatments and the mind and spirit are renewed through pampering indulgences? Or are there deeper healing mechanisms in place that affect people more holistically? Today, as the spa industry has grown to be a mainstream outlet for healing and recreation (Yancey, 2002), and has become a place where people go to seek alternative healing modalities, it is time to truly investigate the claims that the spa industry is making, and to better understand the mechanisms behind what makes a spa experience worthwhile, and why it is so popular.

The spa industry's promotion of healing across "mind, body and spirit" is ubiquitous, but is typically mentioned without definition, detail, or support from scientific study. Research on spa services is scant, and the majority of studies that have been done are based on the physical effects of therapeutic treatments on clinical populations. This gives us some insight into the effectiveness of spa treatments as a form of physical therapy, but does little to attest to the ability of a spa to impact diverse populations, even healthy ones, across mind, body, and spirit. To truly validate this claim we need to review the literature from the field of psychology, and see if contained within, we can find some of the keys to how a spa might have a healing effect on the mental and spiritual domains.

To further understand, and perhaps even enhance the spa's power to generate such a holistic sense of renewal, we can specifically turn to recent research being done in positive psychology, one of the newest branches of psychology. Positive psychology is the science of human flourishing, and as such, is an excellent lens through which to study the realm of spa. Both are committed to helping people maximize their health and happiness, and both are of the belief that health is much more than merely the absence of illness. Positive psychology was founded on the principle that we should focus as much on developing our strengths as we do on correcting our weaknesses (Peterson, 2006), and the popularity of spas in modern society is based on "a growing awareness of the need to build good health –not merely to treat disease" (Yaller & Yaller, 1974, p. 13).

Positive psychology research is focused on the science of human excellence, or understanding ways to increase pleasure, engagement, meaning and spirituality, positive relationships, and developing strengths and virtues (Peterson, 2006). The spa industry, while not as grounded in scientific research, uses similar language to define its own purpose:

> Spa is the love or deeper appreciation of one's self through education, knowledge, and/or wisdom about oneself and one's potential. It is about beauty, health, wellness, fitness, mental health, and spiritual journeys – a time and space for guests to be the best they can be (Johnson & Redman, 2008, p. 6).

Positive psychology, while still a relatively new field, is evidence-based and driven by random assignment, placebo-controlled experiments. This scientific research can help to explain how a spa might be able to renew a person's mind and spirit, and more importantly, how the healing effects of a spa might be enhanced.

CHAPTER 1

The World of Spas

The History of Spa

The origins of the word "spa" are shrouded in mystery. Some say these three letters were scratched onto the walls of ancient roman baths as an acronym for "salude per aqua" or "healing through water" (Johnson & Redman, 2008, p. 38). Others say its roots come from the Walloon word "espa" meaning "fountain," which originated in the Belgian town of Spa, known for its healing thermal springs discovered in the 14th century (van Tubergen & van der Linden, 2002).

Regardless of the origins, throughout the written history of man (and presumably even longer), people have turned to some kind of spa for rituals of healing and cleansing. Historical references track spas back to not only the ancient Romans, but to Sumerian, Egyptian, Hebrew, Greek, Indian and Asian cultures from thousands of years ago (Johnson & Redman, 2008; Yaller & Yaller, 1974). Since ancient times, spas have been centers for healing and have almost always had some connection to the healing properties of water.

Principles of Spa

While the types of spa offerings have varied over the centuries, there do seem to be some basic principles that have been somewhat consistent across the history of spa. First and foremost, spa philosophy is a "holistic" one, in which "the total person" is treated across mental, physical and spiritual domains (Johnson & Redman, 2008, p. 5). Spa treatments tend to be non-invasive and rely on natural remedies to help the body tap into its own healing mechanisms. Health is promoted through heat and water therapies, massage and energy work, herbal remedies, diet and exercise and other forms of "naturopathy" or "healing without drugs or surgery" (Yaller & Yaller, 1974, p. 15). This reliance on "the healing power of nature" and tapping into the body's ability to heal itself has become one of the defining principles of alternative medicine (Marti & Hine, 1995, p. xi).

Spas and Alternative Medicine

Spas have become an important subset of a movement towards "alternative health and medicine" because of the appeal of this naturopathic approach and a growing skepticism of conventional medicine. The role of the physician in alternative medicine is "not to interfere with nature" and to allow natural healing to take place (Kradin, 2008, p. 228). Many conventional medical physicians "are still looking to fix the body as if it were a machine" and since more and more patients are seeking a "whole-person approach" a doctor's visit may lead to "misunderstanding, dissatisfaction, and less than perfect outcomes" (Phalen, 1998, p. 86). There are conditions that traditional medicine is ill prepared to handle that lead to frustration in the therapeutic relationship and send clients looking elsewhere for assistance (e.g., headaches, back pain, chronic conditions, etc.). It is here where an optimistic and professional therapist from an alternative healing style can infuse hope, reduce stress, and create an opportunity for the patient to alleviate the stress response and activate healing (Kradin, 2008). Spas offer a variety of treatments from Eastern and Western traditions that are classified as forms of alternative medicine, including ayurveda, herbal remedies, acupuncture and acupressure, nutrition, exercise, and massage (Marti & Hine, 1995). The continued popularity of alternative healing methods stems not only from a distrust of conventional medicine, but also from "a substantial measure of therapeutic success" that these modalities provide (Kradin, 2008, p. 227).

Even the conventional scientific community is beginning to take alternative medicine more seriously. In an article entitled, "The Triumph of New Age Medicine," author David Freeman outlines the rise in popularity and acceptance for alternative healing methods. "Medicine has long decried acupuncture, homeopathy and the like as dangerous nonsense that preys on the gullible," said Freeman. "But now many doctors admit that alternative medicine seems to do a better job of making patients well, and at a much lower cost, than mainstream care—and they're trying to learn from it" (2011).

Alternative healing methods are more focused on prevention and understanding the root causes of illness rather than "simply suppressing the symptoms," as the role of conventional medicine is sometimes described (Marti & Hine, 1995, p. xii). In the modern, western world, only a small amount of resources are dedicated to the prevention of illness. The vast majority of health care dollars today are spent on expensive treatments and rehabilitation. This is shameful considering that "high-quality preventive interventions have proven efficacious, cost-effective, and enormously more humane than waiting for citizens to develop maladies that medicine and psychology can treat only at very high financial and human costs" (Prilleltensky & Prilleltensky, 2006).

Spas, while offering treatments that are considered therapeutic for certain clinical conditions, primarily serve healthy populations in an attempt to encourage a healthy lifestyle that prevents disease and illness and maintains health and vitality, even as people move through the aging process. Alex Szekely was a spa visionary whose family opened two well-known spas: Rancho La Puerta and the Golden Door, laying the foundation for the modern spa industry that now thrives today in North America (Osborn, 2006). Szekely was known for emphasizing the importance of prevention in spas:

> Picture a dangerous cliff where people are continually falling off and getting hurt. Ambulances come to pick up the injured and take them to the hospital, where high costs are needed to bring them back to health. Now think about how much smarter it would be for someone to build a fence at the top of that cliff – a fence that would prevent people from falling off in the first place. Spas are fences (Ellis, 2004).

Health by Water

The idea of "healing by mineral waters" is another strong underlying principle that can be traced back to every ancient spa culture (Yaller & Yaller, 1974, p. 14). Historical accounts of the uses of water for healing can be found in the histories of Roman baths, English "thermae," indigenous native American "temazcali" or steam bath rituals, Japanese baths or "onsen," or bathing in the waters of sacred rivers such as the river Jordan in Israel (Johnson & Redman, 2008, pp. 40-49).

In the time of Hippocrates (460-370 BC), bathing was considered to be therapeutic and beneficial in the treatment of most diseases. He believed that illness was caused by an "imbalance of the bodily fluids."

Bathing, exercise and massage were thought to be ways to regain balance (van Tubergen & van der Linden, 2002). Historical texts show ancient references to health "resorts" where the sick could go to bathe in healing waters or drink from medicinal fountains (Walton, 1874). This "taking the waters" was considered to be an activity with "deep therapeutic rationales and multifaceted social ramifications" from the times of the Roman Empire through the middle ages and into the modern era (Porter, 1990).

One account described how people would return from these resorts "in a condition notably ameliorated, and are often cured in a manner altogether unexpected" ("Clinique Medicale," Paris, 1865, pp. 58-59 as cited in Walton, 1874). Even the American Medical Association (in 1915) described the curative use of mineral waters as "an established therapeutic custom," saying "the multitudes of persons who indulge in the drinking at the spas, as well as the large number of physicians who repeatedly advise the treatment as an established routine, make it seem more than probable that the practice is a well founded one" (Fitch, 1929, pp. 19-20).

Today, using water for healing is known as "hydrotherapy" and continues to be a prominent part of modern spa offerings. Hydrotherapy has been known for having tremendous therapeutic value in the treatment of a wide variety of ailments, injuries and conditions (Hinsdale, 1910). Healing benefits from hydrotherapy are said to come not only from the mineral content of the water but from "its buoyancy, which makes movement easier, its temperature, which promotes relaxation and decreases pain; its viscosity, which provides resistance so injured patients can maintain muscle tone and aerobic capacity; and its hydrostatic or circumferential pressure, which enhances blood circulation" (Martin & Hine, 1995, p. 16).

The role and importance of water in the spa experience seems to be evolving over time. Historically, "a spa's existence depend[ed] initially on the presence of natural waters and springs in which bodies must be immersed" (Slyomovics, 1993, p. 35). Water continues to be prominent in many modern spas, but it no longer seems to be a requirement or a defining feature. Spas today "subordinate the supposed healing properties of natural water to the benefits of a spiritual and physical discipline" (p. 35). People now seem to believe that the mechanisms behind what makes a spa beneficial go beyond the healing properties of the water.

The Historic Ubiquitousness and Popularity of Spas

Reading descriptions of the Roman baths, where people went "to wash, take exercise, socialize, have a massage or a manicure, or have unwanted hair removed, others went for medical treatment or for advice on dietetics from athletics trainers" (Jackson, 1990, p. 3), one can't help but be amazed at how similar this sounds to the spas of today some two thousand years later. One historian described "the enduring vitality of water treatments and spa regimes over the course of two thousand years" as showing the "lasting faith of the sick" in the healing purity of water treatments (Porter, 1990, p. xi).

Whether spa waters have healing properties or not remains unclear, but what seems to never waver, is the enduring popularity of spas across time and culture. One spa historian described it this way:

> In the heyday of the spa, waters may or may not have cured anyone, but many patients certainly believed they did. They retreated to the waters, they respected these fountains of life, and they celebrated new vigor and youthfulness. If water cured them, no one ever explained why, nor did they need to. Today, there remains the perpetual hope that the Fountain of Youth exists and awaits discovery. We fear aging almost as much as dying. In that way we differ little from our predecessors of the nineteenth century (Valenza, 2000, p. 13).

The popularity of spas has ebbed and flowed intermittently over the past centuries but has never disappeared. The claims of healing by the spa world have not been without controversy. At times, the healing effects of spas have been reduced to "the status of superstition" or considered merely a "social fad" (Howard W. Haggard, M. D., Journal of the American Medical Association, as cited in Valenza, 2000, p. 5). In spite of this, it is the enduring history and ubiquitousness of the spa as a center for health that is the greatest testament to its capacity for healing and for improving the quality of life for its patrons. Reports can be traced back for thousands of years on the contribution of spas "to the prevention of disease, to the improvement and healing of chronic conditions, and to the restoration of health for millions all over the world" (Yaller & Yaller, 1974, p. 14).

The Spa Industry Today

The spa industry today is robust, but not without its challenges. The number of spas has grown substantially in the last ten years (Johnson & Redman, 2008) making the industry more competitive both for customers and for qualified staff. For those looking at alternative ways to improve their health and wellbeing, the spa has been a popular choice. This is evidenced by the massive growth of the industry in the last decade, which has averaged 21% per year since 1999 with revenues now over $9 billion (ISPA, 2007).

In the past, the spa world could be neatly arranged into three buckets: day spas, resort spas and destination spas. Today's spa offerings are so diverse that they are no longer so easily defined. The International Spa Association lists no less than eight categories of spa: club spa, cruise ship spa, cosmetic spa, day spa, destination spa, medical spa, mineral springs spa and resort/hotel spa ("ISPA," 2008). To complicate things further, other businesses are using the "spa" name, so you can drop off your dog at the pet spa, pick up your car from the auto spa and go for your annual teeth cleaning and reflexology at the dental spa. The fastest growing category in the industry is the medical spa, which has its own increasing levels of diversity and can include everything from centers for cosmetic surgery and laser hair removal to complete holistic wellness and weight loss programs supervised by a physician.

While there is no right or wrong way to spa, it is helpful for consumers to understand the core philosophy that has helped to integrate spas into the mainstream. Most of the modern spa offerings available today evolved out of the teachings of the destination spas. Destination spas distinguish themselves from other spas in that the spa is not simply a place to visit while on vacation, but it is the destination in and of itself. The destination spa offers the deepest level of the spa experience, typically inviting people to immerse themselves for at least a week in transformational and nurturing experiences (Johnson & Redman, 2008). These spas do not sell pampering and luxury but rather offer a lifestyle that is drastically different than the way most people live their day-to-day lives. Guests fill their days with activities designed to improve physical conditioning, assess physical and mental health, reflect on values and goals, and learn how to create joy and happiness in their lives. Visiting a destination spa gives people a chance to practice a different kind of lifestyle and learn strategies that they can hopefully apply when they return to the real world.

Much of the research on wellbeing has a clear application in the destination spa setting. In these environments, spas have the luxury of extensive amounts of time with clients where they can really work with them on their health and lifestyle. Over the course of several days, the destination spas have time to help their guests define and clarify their health goals, and not only offer an extensive array of healing services and activities, but also have time to educate their clients via lectures and workshops.

The day spa, which clients can visit for a day or just for an hour, and the hotel/resort spa, where guests can go while traveling and staying at a hotel or resort, are models that have evolved out of the desire to duplicate some of the transformational benefits of a destination spa visit within a much shorter window of time. By giving people the opportunity to take time for themselves in a healing and soothing way, the spas, regardless of type, seek to touch people in a way that extends beyond the confines of their specific treatment. The spa experience shouldn't end when the customer walks out the door. The spa client should leave not only smelling like lavender but with new tools for managing stress, new products and suggestions for self-care, and perhaps even a new perspective on life. Visiting any spa should give at least a taste of the destination spa's transformational menu: fitness concepts, nutritional practices, skin care, active aging, stress relief, mind-body wellness, etc.

The challenge for the spa industry is to find ways to apply the science of wellbeing not only in the extensive offerings of the destination spa but also in the brief windows of time that other types of spas have to interact with clients. Regardless of the type of spa, the biggest value comes from what the customer is able to take away from the experience. Whether it is a new regimen for daily skin care, a new recipe for a healthful meal, or a tip to let go of stress, the spa experience gives people a reminder to value their bodies, their minds and their spiritual wellbeing. It reminds them to take care of themselves.

Pampering and Luxury or Wellness and Essential Self Care?

In recent years, primarily due to the growth of resort and hotel spas, the industry's message has shifted away from wellbeing and towards the idea of pampering and luxury. The spa industry has become virtually synonymous with luxury as spas have become a required amenity in luxury resorts and hotels (Glusac, 2007; Boyd, 2007). Hospitality industry experts have identified "larger and better spas" as one of the biggest trends in the business along with the fact that hotel guests have been "spending a lot more money on spa treatments" (Nardozza, 2007 as cited in Butler, 2007). In this segment of the spa industry, treatments became extremely luxurious, even using caviar and other expensive ingredients in spa products, and spas emphasized luxury and pampering in their marketing messages.

This positioning of spas as an elite activity for wealthy consumers has not been without controversy. The International Spa Association has put out the message that "spas are not about luxury" in an attempt to shift the conversation on the industry back to its roots in wellness. Lynne McNees, president of the association, said, "Spas are about health, reducing stress and aging gracefully" (ISPA, 2009). The spa industry seems to wrestle with its own identity in this respect. The spas want to be taken seriously as centers for health and wellness, but much of their dialogue with consumers is about pampering and luxury.

Pampering as a Part of Wellness

The ideas of pampering and wellness are not mutually exclusive. Rather than criticizing spas for being too pampering, people should ask why they are not pampered in our other healing institutions. Why don't I feel pampered when I visit my doctor's office? Why can't I get five-star customer service when I visit a hospital? These are not "either/or" ideas but "both/and." The spa industry can be about pampering *and* about wellness. Having a unique perspective from working with a luxury clientele, the spa world models a lot of things that our other healing institutions can learn from: they provide lush, comfortable and esthetically pleasing surroundings for their healing experiences, they provide incredibly personal and nurturing services for their clients, and they do it with the highest level of customer service.

Even beauty therapists, who often get a bad rap as being only about "vanity," tend to do a better job than a physician of pampering the clients they are treating. To some, a hair stylist or manicurist may appear to be gossipy, but when interviewed, beauty therapists say they recognize the importance of making their clients "feel loved and interesting" by asking them questions about their personal lives (Sharma & Black, 2001, p. 919). There is a "principle of simultaneity" that suggests that the way interventions are delivered has an effect on the outcome (Cooperrider, Whitney & Stavros, 2008, p. 9). Conventional health care systems could learn a lot from spas in this respect, such as how to deliver healing treatments in a more nurturing way.

While not turning away from their pampering offerings, spas should consider how they can make their services more accessible to a broader, more diverse population of people. The spa industry does invite criticism because of its exclusivity and its focus on the highest spectrum of the socioeconomic scale. There are huge business opportunities for spas that figure out ways to profitably offer their wellbeing services to the larger numbers of people who reside at the base of the economic pyramid. And the individual impact on wellbeing would be magnified if the spa industry could make a greater impact across society (Prilleltensky & Prilleltensky, 2006).

The Role of Spas in Society

The health sciences are converging. The physical, mental and cultural branches of the sciences are recognizing more and more the importance of viewing a person's wellbeing holistically, or across multiple domains. Jonathan Haidt, author of *The Happiness Hypothesis,* called this "cross-level coherence," identifying three levels (physical, mental, and sociocultural) that should be considered when evaluating an individual (2006, p. 227). Spa rituals, for example, are most meaningful when they cohere to all three levels of experience: they are felt viscerally in the physical realm, they are understood conceptually in the mental realm, and they connect to history and tradition in the cultural realm (p. 228).

The ISPA definition of spas emphasizes that spas treat individuals across mind, body and spirit, but does not touch upon the importance of relationships and how they can affect wellbeing as well. The quantity and quality of human relationships is another area that affects wellbeing across all domains, including our overall assessment of how satisfied we are with life (Diener & Biswas-Diener, 2008). "Psychosocial flourishing" occurs when we have healthy relationships that contribute to a positive state of mind (Ryff & Singer, 2002, p. 548). Having quality relationships is "universally endorsed as being central to optimal living" and the lack of them is linked to "increased risk of disease and reduced length of life" (p. 549). Health interventions become more effective when they consider not only physical wellbeing but also "psychological and social flourishing" (Ryff & Singer, 2002). For spas that are truly concerned with wellbeing, they must consider how their clients' relationships and role in society can play a part.

The Role of Society in Health Care

I have defined holistic wellbeing as a philosophy of considering all the parts of an individual across mental, physical and spiritual domains. But another way of looking at holistic wellbeing is to go beyond the individual and consider how wellbeing is affected by the relationships, organizations, communities, societies and systems, to which the individual belongs. The rise of obesity in the United States is an example of a health epidemic that has largely been treated at the individual level. We are now beginning to realize the impact of social and societal factors that are driving this epidemic. New research tells us that obesity spreads through social networks, much like a flu virus would (Christakis & Fowler, 2007; 2011).

Isaac and Ora Prilleltensky, teachers at the University of Miami in Florida, have spent years studying wellness and wellbeing from a community perspective. They classified different wellness interventions along temporal lines (i.e., whether they were more "reactive," as in clinical interventions, or more "proactive," as in preventive interventions) and along ecological lines (i.e., whether they were more geared towards individual change or collective change; Prilleltensky & Prilleltensky, 2006, p. 34).

Spas tend to be more proactive than other health interventions, focusing on prevention and working with healthy populations before they have been afflicted with any kind of ailment. They also tend to be more individual focused, working with "clients" on a one-by-one basis. There is an opportunity for the spa industry to move beyond this individual focus by becoming more involved in finding proactive solutions to wellbeing issues on a community level. "Fixing individuals" without "fixing society" can only get us so far (Smedlye & Syme, 2000 as cited in Prilleltensky & Prilleltensky, 2006, p. 40).

In modern society, most people are not involved in wellbeing decisions on a community-wide scale. The traditional health care system seems to be forced onto individuals without them feeling that they have an active role or a voice in the process. For the most part, citizens are "detached from decision making processes that affect their own health or the health and wellbeing of the entire community" (Prilleltensky & Prilleltensky, 2006, p. 42). Spas should attempt to understand the community and societal factors that contribute to wellbeing, and possibly to play more of a partnering role in working with their clients to resolve issues that impact wellbeing across larger groups of people. By taking a big picture view of the holistic impact of society, community and relationships on wellness, spas could fill a role not being filled by our conventional health care systems and policies.

Spas and Positive Health

The spa industry offering is unique, both due to its holistic approach to wellbeing and because of its emphasis on prevention. The World Health Organization has endorsed these principles when it defined health as a "state of complete physical, mental and social wellbeing and not merely the absence of disease or infirmity" (World Health Organization, 1948, p. 28, as cited in Ryff & Singer, 2002). The spa industry thrives today because of "a growing awareness of the need to build good health –not merely to treat disease" (Yaller & Yaller, 1974, p. 13). The spa industry could play a prominent role in a new field of "positive health" which "encompasses not only physical wellbeing but also psychological and social flourishing" (Ryff & Singer, 2002, p. 548). Positive health is based on the idea that optimal health is more than simply the absence of illness or disease. Spas are aligned with the goal of positive health, which is to maximize human potential and flourishing to achieve optimal health.

Traditionally, health sciences have concentrated on the study and treatment of illness and disease as a way to improve health and wellbeing. In North America, only a small amount of economic resources are allocated to preventative care (Prilleltensky & Prilleltensky, 2006). To a certain extent, investing time, energy and money working on healthy populations seems like a lower priority when there are so many sick people in the world (Seligman, 2008). But proponents of positive health argue that we have an inherent right to push our wellbeing in a positive direction ("above and beyond the relief of their suffering" [p. 5]), regardless of our state of health. Furthermore, focusing on wellbeing in a positive direction could actually be our best defense against illness and disease.

As a new way of looking at health care, positive health will continue to gain traction and momentum. It will be difficult, however, for conventional health care systems to shift gears into the idea of positive health, because they are usually only working with populations that have already slipped into a state of illness, injury or disease and "communication between practitioners and patients is often faulty and aimed at pathology" (Prilleltensky & Prilleltensky, 2006, p. 45). Because spas are providing preventative treatments to a primarily healthy population, they have a unique opportunity to consider their role in ensuring the positive wellbeing of their clients.

To assess the effectiveness of positive health interventions, three different areas of measurement should be considered. Wellbeing can be measured using biological measures (traditional medical tests for illness and other scientific metrics of health), functional measures (ability to work, live, socialize and engage in activity), and subjective measures (a feeling of positive health and wellbeing; Seligman, 2008). For spas to impact their clients' positive health, they should consider how their treatments and services can impact people across all three of these domains.

Spas and Positive Aging

Spas do not always take the most positive approach. For example, spas commonly focus on the negative concept of "anti-aging" in the treatments they offer. Spas have lured people in with statements like, "removes signs of aging," "reduces fine lines and wrinkles," or my personal favorite, "reverses the aging process" (McCarthy, 2008, p. 42). Consumers go to spas offering these anti-aging treatments as one of their ways of struggling mightily against the ravages of time—digging their heels in as deep as they can while they continue to slide forward towards some distant but supposedly gloomy horizon.

In my career, I too have woven these "anti-aging" messages into my spa menus. It has been difficult not to when the consumers are lining up to experience any treatment that will keep them from turning the next corner. People know that certain things will decline as they age: muscle strength, aerobic capacity, sports performance, sexual performance, and overall mobility. But they also know that certain activities in the spa (exercise, for example) can delay or reverse the decline associated with age (R. Fowler, MAPP 700 lecture, November 14, 2008). Spas also offer beauty and skincare treatments, which at least help to maintain the appearance of youth and vitality.

But positive health would suggest that rather than trying to stop or slow down the inevitable process of aging, spas should concentrate on helping people continue to flourish through the aging process. From my perspective, the primary goal of spas is not to make people feel or look younger, but to make them feel *better*. Feeling better is defined as "more happy" and not necessarily as "younger." By fighting the aging process spas are contributing to a form of denial. There really is no such thing as "anti-aging." Aging is a function of time, and until a spa treatment is capable of warping the very fabric of our universe, the aging shall continue. Any attempt to manipulate how someone might move through this process is a struggle against the laws of physics themselves.

In recent years, there has been some movement in the spa industry away from "anti-aging" towards the concept of "active aging" (Brody, 2008). This slight change in semantics has a vast impact on the psychology of the process. The idea is not to fight against aging but to accept and embrace it. By focusing on aging actively, people do not push to reverse the aging process but rather to remain an active participant, and to improve both the quantity and quality of their years. Books like *Younger Next Year* promote the idea of an active lifestyle and the importance of exercise and activity regardless of age (Crowley & Lodge, 2004).

Another positive approach that spas could consider is not anti-aging, not active aging, but *happy aging* (McCarthy, 2008). Isn't that really what people are striving for? Not reversing aging, but aging joyfully. Not active aging, but enjoying each moment regardless of level of activity. Maintaining a high level of activity is not necessarily a universal value. In his book, *Less: Accomplishing More by Doing Less*, author Marc Lesser said,

> Every life has great meaning but the meaning of our own can often be obscured by the fog of constant activity and plain bad habits. . . Doing less leads to more love, more effectiveness and internal calmness, and a greater ability to accomplish more of what matters most (Lesser, as cited by Moody, 2009).

A positive health model encourages us to not only increase the years of our lives, but to increase the quality of the years that we live (Seligman, 2008). This is perhaps best captured by a quotation from the book, *Aging Well*: "Grant unto me the seeing eye, that I may see the beauty in common things . . . and that I may know that each age from first to last is good in itself and may be lived, not only well, but happily" (Edmund Sanford, "Mental Growth and Decay" as cited in Vaillant, 2002, p. 307).

Spas have the potential to help their clients navigate the aging process, not only by helping alleviate the physical aches and pains of aging but also by helping people find psychological wellbeing. In a study of emotions found by analyzing the content of millions of personal blogs posted on the internet, researchers from Stanford University found that the meaning of happiness changed over the course of one's life span. Whereas younger people associate happiness with excitement, older people are more likely to associate happiness with feeling peaceful, suggesting that spas may be a greater source of happiness as people age (Kamvar, Mogilner, & Aaker, 2011). For the younger consumers, spas may be a place to go to learn the joy of peacefulness, an appreciation that will also help them with aging gracefully.

If spas want to assist people with positive aging, they should not only help their clients to maintain physical health and activity, but also help them to increase and express wisdom, experience positive emotions like joy, and have meaningful positive relationships with others (Vaillant, 2002).

CHAPTER 2

Mind, Body, and Spirit in the Spa

Holistic Healing and the Domains of Spa

When spa professionals say that spas enhance wellbeing "through a variety of professional services that encourage the renewal of the mind, body, and spirit," they make a bold claim. While an avid spa-goer may have found the truth in this definition, they represent only a small percentage of the population. For the larger group of peripheral spa-goers, or the even larger segment of the population that has never been to a spa, they may not realize how comprehensive the intentions of the spa industry are. In this book, I review the research and literature from the world of psychology to investigate the possible impact that spas can make on people in this holistic fashion, and to see if there are areas of research that spas could learn from to improve and enhance their offerings.

The world of spa's "holistic" concept of health or "wellness focused on the total person – physical, mental, social, and spiritual" (Johnson & Redman, 2008, p. 5) is what sets spas apart from many other healing institutions in our society. Most medical and natural sciences have traditionally looked exclusively at the physical aspects of wellbeing, while the humanities, "whose literal English translation [from the German word, 'Geisteswissenschaften'] would be 'spiritual (or mental) sciences,'" have traditionally had an antisomatic bias.

Spas recognize that our health cannot be looked at in only one (physical) domain, and so they promise a more holistic approach. The concept of "mind, body and spirit" has become a fundamental part of the language of healing in spas and can be seen woven throughout their mission statements, marketing materials and treatment menus. It is a common belief in the spa industry that the mind, body, and spirit domains are inextricably integrated, and that it would be ineffective to treat a person properly while focusing on only one area. This holistic approach to treating a person across all three of these domains may be what makes the world of spa so appealing as a place for rest and healing.

It is because of this holistic view of health and healing, that the psychological side of the spa experience is so important. Spas need to not only validate the effectiveness and efficacy of treatments for their physical therapeutic value, but also for their healing effect on the mind and the spirit. By investigating the research from the field of psychology, spas can have a greater understanding of how their offerings contribute to holistic wellbeing, and can learn how to develop more and enhanced offerings to encourage renewal in the mental and spiritual domains.

The Philosophy of Mind-Body Healing

The "mind-body problem" is one that has plagued philosophers for centuries. Science has struggled to understand how thoughts, which are ethereal, might manifest themselves in the body. Philosopher Renee ("I think therefore I am") Descartes, considered to be "the father of the mind-body problem," postulated that the mind was completely distinct from the physical world. This became known as "Cartesian Dualism": the concept that "our minds are not our brains" (Audi, 1999, p. 684). Conventional medicine has, for the most part, accepted this hypothesis as fact, treating the body as a type of machine, whose parts can be analyzed, understood, and even removed with little consideration to the role of thoughts, emotions, or consciousness in the process (Phalen, 1998).

Yet we know from our own experience of the world (and from what modern philosophers and scientists are discovering) that there are links between the mental and the physical realm. The five senses are portals through which the physical world is experienced by our mind (Audi, 1994). The concept of tapping in to all five senses is prominent within the spa culture. Spa experiences are filled with rich sensory stimuli in an attempt to cross that mind-body barrier. A typical spa experience may involve tastes, in the form of healthy spa cuisine and/or an herbal elixir before or after treatment; sounds, in the form of relaxing or uplifting music being played during the experience; sights, in the beautiful esthetic design of the spa, which often includes elements of nature; smells, in the aromatherapeutic oils and products being used in treatments; and of course touch, in the massages and other therapies that involve the touch of a nurturing therapist.

People's sensory experience of the world provides input into their minds which is then processed by their thinking and affects their behavior.

While thoughts may be kept in the internal and ethereal realm, they direct our behavior, which defines how we act physically in and on the world. The information between the mental and physical domains is constantly flowing. Spas recognize and embrace this connection and attempt to keep an open awareness between what is going on in the mind and the body.

But spas also need to consider how imperfect the flow of information is between the mind and the body. There are all kinds of mental steps that people undertake when sifting through and processing the enormous amount of information that comes into our mind through our senses. We tend to make several mental errors or get stuck in "thinking traps," which affect how we react to stimuli in the physical world. One way that these reactions are expressed is through emotion (Reivich & Shatte, 2002).

The Emotional Connection between Mind and Body

Our emotions connect the mind and the body because emotions are essentially thoughts that are expressed physically in the body. Some would say the emotions are the "consequences" of certain thoughts or beliefs (Reivich & Shatte, 2002). But while an emotion is a "mental state" it is expressed physically through certain facial expressions, body language, and involuntary physiological reactions brought on by an arousal of the autonomic nervous system (Audi, 1994). Because the emotional side of thoughts is expressed so powerfully in the body, the study of emotions is extremely relevant for understanding holistic wellbeing (Diener & Biswas-Diener, 2008; Fredrickson, 2009; Vaillant, 2008).

Traditionally, most of the research linking emotions and health has focused on negative emotions. Strong connections have been found between the physiological "stress response" and long term health, an area I will be covering more later in the text (Wisneski & Anderson, 2005, p. 76). Recent research also shows a link between positive emotions and health, suggesting that the emotional connections to our physical wellbeing are deeper and more complex than scientists previously imagined (Cohen & Pressman, 2006).

While emotion is not named specifically in the "mind, body, spirit" paradigm, spas have to consider how a person's emotional wellbeing might reside in the link between mind and body. Emotion can also be a component of the spiritual domain since spirituality can be highly emotional and vice versa (Vaillant, 2008).

The Role of the Mind in Holistic Healing

American psychologist and philosopher William James (1842-1910) often referred to a system of beliefs known as "mind cure" that was effective in improving wellbeing: "blind have been made to see, the halt to walk; lifelong invalids have had their health restored. The moral fruits have been no less remarkable" (1985, p. 84). Often, the mechanism behind an effective health intervention is the ability to tap into the powers of the mind to improve health and subjective state.

Mental training can have a positive impact on the physical domain, as in the athlete's ability to focus attention so that his thoughts enable the right actions. It is the athlete's mental training that tells him "keep your eye on the ball" while simultaneously quieting unnecessary thoughts that could detract from his coordination to let his body swing away. Some have even suggested that the mind evolved specifically as a tool to coordinate movement in the body (Ratey & Hagerman, 2008). Furthermore, mental awareness of our physical states such as consciousness of breath, "can inform us that we are anxious or angry when we might otherwise remain unaware of these emotions and thus more vulnerable to their misdirection" (Shusterman, 2006, p. 12).

An example of mental training that is taught in spas is the practice of meditation. The purpose of meditation is to improve mental wellbeing by developing "optimal openness, awareness, and insight" (Shapiro, Schwartz & Santerre, 2002, p. 634). Research has discovered outcomes from meditation that can be measured physiologically, such as a relaxed physical state, release of hormones associated with positive mood, and a decreased reaction to stress. One study of people with consistently high health care costs found that a long-term practice of Transcendental Meditation led them to a 28% reduction in physician fees (Herron, 2011). Research on positive emotions has found that meditation is a reliable way to increase people's "positivity ratio," and that much of the benefits of meditation could be attributed to the concurrent increase in positive feelings (Fredrickson, 2009). Another study showed significantly higher scores on a measure of spirituality after practicing mindfulness meditation. Meditation is an example of an intervention which impacts "physiological, psychological, and transpersonal wellbeing:" body, mind and spirit (p. 638).

Psychologists have long ago identified the importance of the mind-body connection in psychosomatic healing and have learned that "how we think and feel will affect the functioning of the body" (Mutrie & Faulkner, 2004, p. 147). Research also supports the existence of "a strong relationship between physical activity and psychological wellbeing." The relationship goes both ways since physical health helps to enhance mental health outcomes which in turn "motivate people to persist in physical activity," an upward spiral which suggests physical activity can be exponentially beneficial (p. 148).

Physical Fitness and Exercise

The spa industry encourages physical exercise and movement as an important part of a healthy lifestyle. Spas often offer fitness facilities including equipment for cardiovascular training, strength training and balance training, and may offer classes in a variety of movement exercises as well as provide personal training and other workshops to help people increase the level of activity in their lives. Fitness is considered a necessary part of the spa philosophy and lifestyle, despite the fact that this is not typically a large source of revenues for the spa industry.

The physical benefits of fitness training are widely accepted. Physical inactivity is known to be "the biggest public health problem of the 21st century" (Blair, 2009, p. 1). Exercise has been said to be "the central ingredient to good health" (Fries & Vickery, 2001, p. 4). Exercise lowers the risk of heart disease and death, improves immune system functioning, improves cardiovascular functioning and also reduces stress which is associated with a host of negative health implications (R. Fowler, MAPP 700 lecture, November 14, 2008). Activity levels are inversely related, for example, to the rates of developing certain kinds of cancer such as breast, colon and prostate cancer (Ratey & Hagerman, 2008 p. 84). In general, exercise is widely considered to be the best way to extend both the quantity and quality of the years of your life. Most of the advice from the book, *Younger Next Year*, can be summed up in a single sentence: "Exercise [hard] six days a week for the rest of your life" (Crowley and Lodge, 2004, p. 49).

Increasingly, fitness is thought to be important not only for the physical realm but across all domains of the individual. Exercise is good for physical health, which in turn is a driver of "psychological wealth" (Diener & Biswas-Diener, 2008). Physically fit people tend to be both healthier and happier (R. Fowler, MAPP 700 lecture, November 14, 2008). And exercise is often the best prescription as a substitute to replace other less healthy behaviors (Prochaska, Norcross, Diclemente, 1994). So how does exercise and physical activity have such an impact on mind and spirit?

Somaesthetics

"Somaesthetics" is a term coined by Richard Shusterman to elevate the importance of awareness and use of the body in people's lives, for reasons that go beyond mere physical health. As a relatively new branch of the sciences, somaesthetics seeks to merge the physical with the mental/spiritual, and could help to bring validity to the spa industry's philosophy of holistic healing. Like the spa industry, somaesthetics recognizes that the body is connected to the mental because it is the "transparent source of perception . . . *from which* and *through which*" the world is perceived, allowing cognition and observation to occur (Shusterman, 2006).

Shusterman described a variety of somatic interventions that affect people not only physically, but across the mental and spiritual domains as well (2006). The somaesthetic principles dictate somatic training not only for physical health but to improve wisdom and virtue, "by giving us greater perceptual sensitivity and powers of action." For example, somaesthetics recognizes many of the activities commonly offered in spas aimed at "instilling proper body-mind harmony" such as yoga, meditation, martial arts, and breathing exercises (p. 8).

"Pragmatic somaesthetics" is the critical and comparative study of various somatic methods designed to remake the body including grooming, diets, meditative and martial arts, aerobics, massage, bodybuilding and modern psychosomatic disciplines such as Alexander Technique and Feldenkrais Method (p. 14) all of which can be found in select spas. We can also distinguish between "holistic" or "experiential" methods, which are "systems of somatic postures and movements to develop the harmonious functioning and energy of the person as an integrated whole" (e.g., yoga, tai chi and Feldenkrais) and "atomistic" or "representational" methods, which are aimed at specific areas of the body and concerned primarily with outward appearances (e.g., Salon and beauty treatments or other cosmetic treatments such as laser hair removal and/or plastic surgery; p. 14). Some spas are criticized as offering only superficial beauty treatments, but a somaesthetic approach would value the connections between looking good, feeling good and being well.

Inner and Outer Dimensions of Holistic Wellbeing

One way that the holistic (mind, body, spirit) philosophy is expressed in the spa industry is through beauty treatments designed to make people feel better by helping them to look their best. Spas offer nutritional and exercise programs as well as a variety of grooming and beauty services (haircuts, styling and coloring, manicures and pedicures, hair removal, makeup, skincare, etc.). Even the most apparently superficial of spa beauty treatments can have meaningful and positive psychological impacts.

For example, in one recent study of a six-month weight-loss program, The Society for the Study of Ingestive Behvior found that participants lowered their weight by 8%, reduced risk factors for heart disease and stroke, experienced improved mood and even reduced symptoms of depression. This was an unusual finding since depressive subjects are usually excluded from weight loss research, leading the researchers to suggest further studies on the use of weight loss as a way of treating psychiatric disorders (Faulconbridge, et al., 2009).

Another recent study on "Botox" (Botulinum Toxin A injection) treatments found that the injections reduced signs of depression, anxiety and irritableness (theoretically by reducing clients' abilities to frown; Lewis & Bowler, 2009). Based on research like this, a hospital in Switzerland is now doing clinical trials on the use of Botox for treatment of depression (Wollmer, 2009).

Most employees in the spa industry are well aware of the psychological impact of their work. A research study on beauty therapists in the United Kingdom found that they "defined beauty therapy in terms of work with *feelings* as well as with the *body*" (Sharma & Black, 2001, p. 914).

Even a spa service as simple as tweezing a client's eyebrows cannot be isolated to only the physical domain since "how we look influences how we feel, and vice versa" (Shusterman, 2006, p. 15). The beauty therapists interviewed in the study above felt that the thing that tied together all of their diverse service offerings was that they were "all trying to make people feel better . . . making people feel better, giving people confidence" (Sharma & Black, 2001, p. 918).

Somaesthetics recognizes that these "representational" (outer) dimensions of somatic activities can supplement and enhance the "experiential" (inner) dimensions. Spa clients, for example, may start a diet or exercise program exclusively for representational reasons, to improve their outward appearance. But over time they may find that the experiential component of these activities becomes even more rewarding (Shusterman, 2006).

These are not mutually exclusive dimensions; most somatic exercises will have both representational (outer) and experiential (inner) dimensions. Representational activities such as dieting or bodybuilding "often produce inner feelings that are then sought for their own experiential sake" (p. 15). Put simply, exercising the body benefits not only the outward appearance and physical health, but psychological wellbeing as well (Mutrie & Faulkner, 2004).

Many of the research findings on the link between physical activity and psychological wellbeing come from clinical populations (those battling with depression for example.) There seems to be a two way relationship here in that physically active people are less likely to get depressed and depressed people are less likely to exercise (R. Fowler, MAPP 700 lecture, November 14, 2008). In some studies, prescribed exercise has proven to be more effective than medication in the treatment of depression (Ratey & Hagerman, 2008). Many experts now suggest combining exercise with medication for the most effective treatment. Exercise serves as the second "medication" for people with depression (Trivedi, et al., 2011).

Psychological Benefits of Exercise

One explanation for the psychological benefits of exercise is the release of hormones such as endorphins into the bloodstream. These neurotransmitters are known to not only relieve pain, but also induce good feelings (also known as the "runner's high"; Ratey & Hagerman, 2008, p. 118). Studies have shown that even a single bout of exercise for as little as ten minutes can have a positive impact on vigor and mood in healthy subjects. But there seems to be more to the story than this because exercise not only makes you feel good, it also makes you "feel good *about* yourself" (p. 118) by improving self-esteem, which is also associated with psychological health (R. Fowler, MAPP 700 lecture, November 14, 2008).

Physical activity has been recognized as an effective treatment for psychological disorders since the nineteenth century as evidenced by the following quotation from a treatment program for alcoholism which seemed to follow a spa-like regime:

The benefits accruing to the patients from the well-directed use of exercise and baths is indicated by the following observed symptoms: increase in weight, greater firmness of muscles, better colour of skin, larger lung capacity, more regular and stronger action of the heart, clearer action of the mind, brighter and more expressive eye, improved carriage, quicker responses of nerves, and through them of muscle and limb to stimuli. All this has become so evident to them that only a very few are unwilling to attend the classes and many speak freely of the great benefits derived (Cowles, 1898 as cited in Mutrie & Faulkner, 2004, p. 150).

Like visiting a spa, people often say that they exercise, "because it makes me feel good" (Mutrie & Faulkner, 2004, p. 152). Those good feelings that exercise brings can last long after the exercise session is over, motivate positive health behaviors in the future, and improve the quality of life. Exercise has a small but consistently positive effect on mood and is related to reduced anxiety, increased self-esteem and healthy sleep patterns.

The newest research in exercise science suggests that one of the ways activity may boost psychological wellbeing is by leading to improvements in cognitive functioning (Mutrie & Faulkner, 2004; Ratey & Hagerman, 2008). Physical movement is crucial to brain development in part because everything the mind processes comes through the sensory systems of the body (Shusterman, 2006) and also because a large part of brain functioning is centered around coordinating the movement of the body. Physical activity stimulates brain proteins that encourage the brain to grow, literally growing new neurons and then helping them to bind to one another to foster communication throughout the nervous system (Ratey & Hagerman, 2008). Aerobic exercise has been shown to improve cognitive functioning in adults, and older adults who exercise are less likely to develop dementia. 45 minutes of rapid walking three times a week was found to improve reasoning, decision making and working memory (R. Fowler, MAPP 700 lecture, November 14, 2009). Physical activity, especially when it involves complex motor skills, challenges the brain as well as the body, and fosters healthy growth and development in both (Ratey & Hagerman, 2008).

Spas should consider how this information can be used to educate and motivate different populations regarding the importance of physical activity. It is common knowledge that exercise is important to maintain physical health, but it is revolutionary to learn the impact that exercise has on human brain functioning as well as on levels of overall happiness, self-esteem and subjective wellbeing. Some people (e.g., those who are more cerebral by nature) may not value the importance of exercise based on its physical benefits. But the fact that exercise plays a positive role in our cognitive functioning and memory as we age is a powerful motivator that can be used to get different populations into the gym (Ratey & Hagerman, 2008).

Physical activity as a way to holistic wellbeing is also consistent with Deci and Ryan's view (1985) that autonomy, control and relatedness are key ingredients of human flourishing. Developing physical strength gives people a sense of autonomy and control that can improve their satisfaction with life. And since much physical activity occurs within the context of supportive group environments, it gives enhanced opportunities for positive social interaction which bring more positive emotions and a deeper sense of meaning (Mutrie & Faulkner, 2004).

Spirituality in Spas

Since psychology is the "study of the mind," it is easy to see how a look at this research can assist with a greater understanding of how spas impact mental renewal and wellbeing. But what is the "spirit" part of the mind-body-spirit triad? And how do spas impact people's spiritual wellbeing? These are not easy questions to answer since spirit could be defined in many ways and may even be perceived differently from spa to spa or from individual to individual. But there is something about the spiritual side of the world of spas that speaks to people, and keeps them coming back for more.

Spirit as Emotion

For some, spirit can be defined as the emotional side of wellbeing. George Vaillant, a research psychiatrist and professor at Harvard University defined spirituality as "an amalgam of the positive emotions that bind us to other human beings" (2008, pp. 4-5). Some people may identify their spiritual wellbeing with their emotional state, which could reside anywhere on a continuum from "depression" to "elevation." As mentioned previously, this emotional aspect of spirit is not independent from the mind-body connection, since emotions are stimulated by beliefs and cognitions in the mind and are expressed viscerally in the body (Haidt, 2006).

Candace Pert, a pharmacologist, is known for her theories on the "molecules of emotion," which she described as "the link between the physical body and nonphysical states of consciousness" (Pert, 2006, p. 31).

It is common to hear of people experiencing an emotional release while at the spa, sometimes even bursting into tears on the treatment table, perhaps moved by the nurturing touch of the therapist. Guests who have this experience feel a soothing of the spirit, and they leave the spa emotionally at peace, with fewer troubles, less anxiety, and more happiness. Pert teaches that releasing emotions is a critical part of the healing process (Pert, 1997).

For most spas providing holistic treatments and experiences, they strive to not only encourage physical and mental health, but to release pent up emotional wounds and to elevate clients' moods while doing so (an area where other healing institutions such as hospitals, clinics, and doctors' offices could learn something from spas). According to Vaillant, "positive emotions cannot be distinguished from what people understand as spirituality" (2008, p. 15).

Spirit as Energy

For others, the spirit in the spa may be more about energy. Several traditional spa treatments from a variety of cultures are designed to promote the healthy flow of energy in the body. This life force or energy has different names such as "ki" in Japanese Reiki, "chi" in Chinese energy exercises such as chi gung or tai chi, or "prana" (which is also related to the breath) in Sanskrit yoga traditions. The latin word "spiritus" means breath, so it is not surprising that breath is a key component to these energy modalities, which promote healing and rejuvenation, literally revitalizing the spirit ("Ch'I," 2009).

Spirit as Soul

Some spas are even so bold as to suggest that the spirit part of the spa triad refers to the soul. This is not too surprising since "spirit" is often defined as that which connects us to something greater than ourselves, or to "the divine spark in each human being" (Campbell & Brennan, 1994, p. 202). It is not uncommon to see spas promoting their "soul soothing" treatments or using "mind, body and soul" as a substitute for mind, body and spirit. Scientists argue whether or not there is even any difference between the concepts of "soul" and "spirituality" and the emotional limbic system that drives much of our behavior (Vaillant, 2008). From a scientific perspective, the emotional definition of spirituality above may apply just as well when we substitute the word "soul."

It may feel like a stretch to imagine that spas can play a role in our spiritual salvation, but it is not entirely out of the question when you consider the space and time provided at spas for personal reflection. Spas and churches may be the only two places left in our society where we are forced to separate from technology and spend some time in silent reflection. Kenneth Pargament, psychology professor at Bowling Green State University who specializes in the psychology of religion, defined spirituality as "the search for the sacred" (Pargament & Mahoney, 2009, p. 1). In his definition, the term "search" indicates that "spirituality is a process" and is unique to each individual. The term "sacred" represents the substance of our spiritual journey and could include concepts of God or "transcendent reality." Like beauty, transcendence is in the eye of the beholder, so people can find sanctity in many areas of their life including their work, their relationships, their time, or their community. Within the context of this secular definition, it is easier to see the spiritual side of the spa.

For some, the human body is sacred and the rituals performed in the spa are designed to honor that sanctity by improving health, healing, and physical relaxation. The human body is relevant to our moral health because it acts as "the essential medium or tool through which [social norms and moral values] are transmitted, inscribed, and preserved in society." Our ethical life "is grounded in the body" because every moral decision requires a physical action in order for it to be realized. Even "transcendence" or "the urge to reach beyond oneself" is expressed physically as the body reaches out for ever-increasing vitality via a connection with the world through food, sex, and self-transformational activity (Shusterman, 2006).

For people who hold their relationships with others as sacred, the spa provides a place where they can come together and deepen their connections. And perhaps the most sacred concept in the spa is the importance of time for one's self. By giving people time to slow down, be separated from technology, and sit in silence, spas give them a chance to reflect on the values that are most important to them.

CHAPTER 3

Spas and the Psychology of Wellbeing

Psychology of Spa

The people who work with me in the hotel and spa industry are sometimes baffled by my studies in psychology. They often ask if I am leaving hospitality industry to pursue a career in psychology. But for me, psychology and spas and hospitality are inextricably intertwined. Perhaps it is because I have spent my lifetime studying psychology, but I see visits to a spa as a psychological event. This is evidenced by the kinds of feedback I have received from customers over twenty years of working in spas. Typically, the extremely good or extremely bad feedback does not have anything to do with the facilities of the spa, or even with the treatments themselves. It has to do with how we made them feel (good or bad), usually based on their interactions with one of our employees.

The Physical Benefits of Spa

When people think of visiting a spa, they immediately think of the physical benefits. Massage, the most popular treatment in the spa, loosens up the tissues of the body by manipulating the skin, muscles and fascia. Massage and other touch therapies have been used by cultures from around the world for thousands of years as a means of healing, managing pain and relieving stress (Field, 1996). Hippocrates, in 400 B.C. defined medicine as "the art of rubbing" and "rubbing was the primary form of medicine until the pharmaceutical revolution of the 1940s" (Field, 1998, p. 1270). Massage today, while popular, is considered an "alternative" form of therapy, and the research on it is limited, typically using small sample sizes, and focused on clinical conditions (p. 1270).

Massage has been shown to decrease blood pressure, reduce stress, relieve pain, relieve swelling and even have an impact on the cellular level (Kaye, Kaye, Swinford, Baluch, Bawcom, Lambert & Hoover, 2008). Massage is said to be good for circulation, promoting venous and lymphatic drainage. It is also good for the nervous system, releasing hormones that reduce pain, alleviate anxiety, and support the immune system (Wisneski & Anderson, 2005; Kendall-Reed & Reed, 2004). Across a variety of studies massage has been shown to decrease anxiety, depression and stress hormones such as cortisol (Field, 1998). In some studies, benefits were seen in Swedish massage sessions as short as six minutes long (Kaye, Kaye, Swinford, Baluch, Bawcom, Lambert & Hoover, 2008).

In addition to massage, spas offer a variety of natural therapies, including nutrition, supplements, exercise, herbal remedies, and mind/body movement such as yoga. The goal of these kinds of therapies is to "restore biological balance in the body by altering hormone levels, enzymes, blood sugar, and neurotransmitters in order to re-establish a homeostatic balance (Kendall-Reed & Reed, 2004, p. 123). At a spa, people can have a massage to improve circulation and release toxins in the body; they can try a body or facial treatment using a variety of creams, lotions and masks with curative properties designed to rejuvenate and nourish the skin; they can use hydrotherapy to improve circulation; or they can start an exercise program or a healthy diet. It is easy to see and understand the physiological benefits of the many spa offerings.

The Science of Spa

The Global Spa Summit has just launched a new website, http://www.spaevidence.com, which serves as a portal into databases of medical research on spa and wellness therapies. From my years in the spa industry, I can tell you that the people behind this industry passionately believe in the services they offer and their potential impact on human wellbeing. I can also tell you, that the spa industry has not been taken seriously by health care practitioners (in spite of a massive trend towards the "spaification" of health care.)

This is a huge step forward for the spa industry, as the website serves to validate much of what the spa industry has to offer and can help to educate health care practitioners, consumers, and spa professionals themselves, on the research behind what they do. Nobody can say it better than Daniel Friedland of SuperSmartHealth, one of the advisors on the project:

> Conventional medicine, no doubt, has a lot to offer, particularly for patients who are struggling to manage and cure disease. The Spa and Wellness Industry has an immense amount to offer too, especially around maintaining wellness and preventing disease, as well as providing healing and benefit with various wellness modalities to health seekers who are navigating their disease.
>
> The portal provides more than scientific validation around the value of various Spa and Wellness modalities. It is also a gateway through which many who have been laboring for so long with love and deep conviction, experience an emotional catharsis in discovering their life's work validated and their purpose emboldened with meaning and significance (Ellis, 2011).

This new initiative does give me a sense that the spa industry has reached a turning point.

I believe in scientific exploration as a means to deepen our understanding, and spa professionals should be aware of the research behind their modalities. But I also think it's possible for the spa industry to be *too scientific*. After all, we already have tons of health care institutions that are offering scientifically validated treatments. The value of the spa industry is that they go beyond science, offering services that are more holistic and encompassing the psychological and spiritual aspects of wellbeing (where the science is less clear). And the spa industry offers experiences that are novel, nurturing and pampering i.e., the delivery of the interventions is enjoyable, something we don't get from our other more scientifically validated healing institutions.

But that being said, we shouldn't ignore what science has to offer. We should learn from research that has been done and push the boundaries to continue widening the circle of our scientific understanding of holistic wellbeing. We just also need to recognize the limitations of science and not be afraid to go beyond the boundaries of that understanding. To quote psychologist Todd Kashdan, "we should be guided by our science but not governed by it" (2011).

My only complaint about the Spa Evidence portal is that it does not include the PsycINFO database, which would include a broader collection of psychological research on spa modalities. If the spa industry is to stay true to its holistic roots and not fall into the same trap in healthcare of looking only at the physical nature of our interventions, then we must consider research being done beyond the physical domain.

An important aspect of the portal is that its intention is not to only post research that supports the modalities that spas offer but also to house research that might refute or contradict the benefits of certain spa offerings (ear candling anyone?) This gives me hope that the tool will not only be used as a marketing tool for the spa industry, but as a true portal to greater understanding about different pathways to wellbeing.

Whether you are a spa professional interested in learning more about the science of spas and wellbeing, a consumer curious about how spa modalities might be of benefit to you, or a health care practitioner wondering how spa services or partnerships might integrate with your practice to improve results, visit http://www.spaevidence.com and browse through the databases. It is easy to use, very educational, and could help bring spa and healthcare closer together.

The Psychological Impact of Spa

The PsycINFO database has tons of research on mind-body modalities such as mindfulness, meditation, tai chi, Reiki, stress relief, as well as looking at psychological outcomes of massage, exercise, nutrition, yoga and more. I've discussed this with some members of the board of Global Spa Summit and I think they are open to including this as a future enhancement to the spaevidence.com website.

This is important because in addition to providing therapeutic benefits in the physical realm, the spa industry claims their treatments can also be *psychologically* beneficial, improving your mental and spiritual wellbeing. Spas are said to "encourage the renewal of mind, body and spirit" (Johnson & Redman, 2008, p. 12) and the spa industry does not take this claim lightly. While they recognize the "sheer enjoyment of going to a spa and receiving services," they also see spas as a place of healing, offering the key elements of a healthy lifestyle, including "nutritious food, fitness activities, face and body treatments, medical evaluations, behavioral management counseling, nutrition education, stress management, holistic health, spiritual growth, movement therapy, exercise physiology, and more" (p. 11).

Besides feeling good, how else do all of these services impact holistic wellbeing? For the most part, the treatments appear to be primarily physical in nature: massage is a physical manipulation of the tissues of the body; facials and skincare include more superficial treatments for the skin, one of the most important organs of the body; hydrotherapy involves using heat, water and steam to loosen up body tissues and improve circulation. What do any of these physical therapies have to do with mind and spirit?

We have already seen how the spa philosophy emphasizes the connection between mind and body in healing. Some bodywork techniques have evolved to specifically address the relationship between mind and body. Rolfing and the Trager method are two examples of bodywork therapies that work on "the correlation between manipulation of the body and the releasing of deep emotions" (Wisneski & Anderson, 2005, p. 151). All of the physical spa therapies listed above are designed to not only create healthy physiological changes in the body, but also to bring mental relaxation and psychological harmony. The mental and physical natures of these therapies "are intimately intertwined and often overlap" (Kendall-Reed & Reed, 2004, p. 123). There may be more to the spa experience than can be easily detected by only examining the physical realm. The scientific literature from the field of psychology can illuminate some of the "hidden" mechanisms that may be amplifying the beneficial effects of spa therapies and explaining the role they can play in the psychological domain.

The Effect of Person

Some of the most interesting findings from the new field of positive psychology have been summed up by the simple statement, "other people matter" (Peterson, 2006). In medicine, the influence of the doctor on his patient has been recognized since the time of Hippocrates, and is often cited as one of the greatest drawbacks to the "disappearance of the family physician" (Anderson & Gantt, 1966, p. 181). Researchers have also cited that there are "many other examples of assuaging influence of one person on another" (p. 181) and studies on "social support" have found the mitigating effect of good relationships with other people on the harmful effects of stress (Acuna & Bruner, 2002). One way that spas provide healing across mind, body and spirit is by the presence of a nurturing therapist.

The importance of the therapist in the spa setting can be easily noted by considering the difficulty for someone to get as much enjoyment out of massaging their own muscles as they do when the therapy is being done by someone else. The effects of touch may be amplified when they come from another person. The touch of another person can be healing in a way that a person touching themselves cannot achieve much in the way that a person can't tickle themselves (Sapolsky, 2004, p. 336). The touch and nurturing care of another person is an important mechanism in the subjective benefits of a visit to a spa.

Most people are aware of the famous psychological conditioning experiments involving Pavlov's dog. By associating a bell with food, a dog would learn to salivate at the sound of the bell. Similar experiments have been done with flashing lights and electric shock, showing that the dogs' fear reactions (heart rate, etc.) would amp up as soon as the light flashed. Most people don't know about the "effect of person" that has also been found in these studies (Anderson & Gantt, 1966; Lynch, 2000). The presence of a researcher in the room with the dog had a calming effect. Their heart rate did not go up as quickly, and returned to normal much sooner whenever there was a person in the room. The effect of a nurturing therapist taking care of a guest in a spa treatment may begin before they even set their hands on them. Some of the "energy" spa treatments, such as Reiki, Therapeutic Touch and craniosacral are deeply rooted in this philosophy.

There is research suggesting the presence of a person can have "marked effects on the heart rate of another person" (Whitehorn, Kaufman & Thomas, 1935 as cited in Gantt, Newton, Royer & Stephens, 1966, p. 31). And studies have shown the positive effects of "contact comfort" of another person on stress levels (Bridger and Birns, 1963; Geer and Turteltaub, 1967; Jones, 1924; Schachter, 1959 as cited in Gattozzi, 1971, p. 181). Darwin once described a heart patient with an irregular pulse rate which "invariably became regular as soon as my Father entered the room" (1955 as cited in Gantt, Newton, Royer & Stephens, 1966, p. 32). Another doctor wrote of his amazement as a dying patient's heart rate and heart rhythm changed "just as soon as a nurse began to hold his hand shortly before his death" (p. 213). What amazed him was that his patient was in a deep coma and should have been completely unaware of the presence of the nurse.

From as far back as 2,000 years ago, doctors have documented cardiac reactions to brief, transient human interactions. Sometimes these effects can be negative, as in the increased heart rate and blood pressure caused by the stress of being evaluated by a doctor (known as "white-coat hypertension"; Lynch, 2000, p. 217). Heart rate studies of psychotherapy sessions have shown a concomitant "cardiac relationship" between the patient and the therapist when they were communicating well (p. 218). The "effect of person" could explain why different styles of psychotherapy all seem to have similar positive results, regardless of the specific techniques being used (Luborsky, 1975 as cited in Prochaska, Norcross & Diclemente, 1994). "The quality of the relationship" seems to matter more than the technique employed by the therapist (Shannon, 2002). And military specialists since World War II have observed the importance of relationships in helping soldiers cope with battle stress. This phenomenon has been replicated in laboratory settings, where experiments have shown that people prefer not to be alone when confronting a stressful situation (Lynch, 2000).

The Power of Touch

In the spa setting, not only do people benefit from the presence of another person, whose role is to nurture and care for you, but those benefits are deepened because they are transmitted through touch. Those same studies on "effect of person" show that the relaxation effect on the dogs is greatly enhanced when the dog is being petted by a human being. Even when the dog is aware of an impending electrical shock, the gentle petting of a researcher can help their heart rate go *down* rather than up (Lynch, 2000). Pavlov called this a "social reflex" noting that different dogs had different reactions to different researchers, depending on the specific relationship the dog had with each individual (1928 as cited in Gantt, Newton, Royer & Stephens, 1966, p. 18). Other research has shown changes in heart rate and behavior in dairy cows influenced by human stroking of the skin (Schmied, Waiblinger, Scharl, Leisch & Bovin, 2007).

One study found that having pets was one of the strongest predictors of survival one year after release from a coronary care unit (p. 240), presumably due to the companionship, sense of purpose, and affectionate touch that pets provide. Another study showed that small children were more likely to smile and reach for live animals (i.e., the family pet) then they were a mechanized version of the animal (Kidd & Kidd, 1987). Psychologists (who are notorious for stressing out mice and rats in lab experiments) have found that handling rats when they are young makes them more resilient to stress as they grow older (Meaney, Aitken, Bhatnager, van Berkel & Sapolsky, 1988, as cited in Sapolsky, 2004). In the wild, a follow up study showed that rats that are licked and groomed by their mothers are also better able to withstand the effects of stress as they get older (Liu et al., 1997, as cited in Sapolsky, 2004).

Even Darwin, in his work on the evolution of the animal kingdom, found that touch had a powerful influence. Certain animals had a "strong desire to touch the beloved person . . . Dogs and cats manifestly take pleasure in rubbing against their master and in being rubbed . . . Monkeys delight in fondling and in being fondled" (1955 as cited in Gantt, Newton, Royer & Stephens, 1966, p. 32). He described human expressions of affection as being innate "insofar as it depends on the pleasure derived from contact with the beloved person."

While research on humans is not as easy to find, there are studies in the literature of the importance of touch to newborns and childhood development. Touch is the first of the senses to develop (and it lasts "even after seeing and hearing begin to fade"; Field, 1994, p. 8). Cases of "psychosocial dwarfism" are found in institutionalized children who have all their physiological needs met and yet find their growth stunted due to the lack of a loving caretaker (Harrington, 2002; Field, 1994).

Studies in Uganda show that the way parents carry their children helps them to develop and learn to walk more quickly. And parents massaging their infants brings the parents and children closer together in a way that few other activities can, while also helping their parents to become familiar with their children's bodies. Touch helps not only with growth and development, but also gives reassurance and self-esteem (Field, 1994). "A child's first emotional bonds are built from physical contact, laying the foundation for further emotional and intellectual development" (p. 9).

One study showed that hand-holding helped to calm the nerves of people anticipating an electric shock. The effect was greatest when holding their spouse's hand, but even holding a stranger's hand was more calming than no hand-holding whatsoever (Coan, Schaefer & Davidson, 2006). Other couples research showed how positive physical contact lowered their cortisol and heart rate responses to stress while verbal social support did not (Ditzen et al., 2007). Another study done with married couples showed that "warm touch" behaviors between spouses had beneficial effects on many stress-related health systems including blood pressure and levels of cortisol and oxytocin (Holt-Lunstad, Birmingham & Light, in press).

Oxytocin, which is "released in the brain in response to social contact, especially skin-to-skin touch" is a hormone-like substance that seems to provide the biochemical basis for love emotions (Insel, 1997 as cited in Peterson, 2006, p. 249). Oxytocin may be one of the mechanisms that make touch not only reduce the heart rate, but also levels of hormones such as cortisol that are associated with the stress response (Ditzen et al., 2007). As one expert on touch therapies said, "Given that most diseases are exacerbated by stress and that massage therapy alleviates stress, receiving massages should probably be high on the health priority list, along with diet and exercise" (Field, 1996, p. 320).

This research suggests that some of the benefits of massage therapies may come simply from the body's physiological reaction to human touch. The power of touch to heal is not a new phenomenon of the modern spa industry. Stories of healers using the "laying on of hands" are found in most religious texts from across cultures and throughout recorded history (Field, 1994). It has been said to be "one of the oldest and most persistent treatments, still used today." References to the "royal touch" in which a King or other person of power heals by touching can be found from as far back as 300 B. C. (Shapiro & Shapiro, 1997, p. 17).

Studies have shown that superficial touch is almost as effective as deep tissue massage in relieving pain as compared to a control group, suggesting that much of the benefits of massage could come simply from touch. This could be attributed to the "placebo effect" with the superficial touch giving the client a greater expectation that a treatment is occurring as compared to a "no-treatment" control group. But it could also be an indication of the oxytocin producing, stress relieving effects of light touch that has been shown in numerous studies. The release of oxytocin is facilitated by touch and this hormone has been shown to increase pain threshold, relieve pain, induce physical relaxation, and lower blood pressure (Law, Evans, Knudtson, Nus, Scholl & Sluka, 2008).

One study attempted to compare massage and simple touch on their ability to enhance mood and reduce pain in advanced stage cancer patients. Patients in both the massage and the touch groups showed improvement both in mood and pain levels showing that the benefits may have come less from the physical manipulation of the body tissues and more from the attention and touch of a nurturing therapist (Kutner, Smith, Corbin, Hemphill, Benton, Mellis, Beaty, Felton, Yamashita, Bryant & Fairclough, 2008). Even in psychological therapies, where touch has traditionally been taboo--a violation of the boundaries of trust between the patient and the therapist--it is becoming more accepted to recognize touch as an effective therapy for "promoting, nurturing, and enhancing emotional expression" (LaTorre, 2005, p. 185).

The effects of people and touch become even more relevant for people who are experiencing or recovering from heart problems. Dr. James J. Lynch, who has done substantial research on "the medical consequences of loneliness," said that "the importance of human touch in such circumstances ought not to be minimized: human contact can serve as one of the primary healing agents for the injured heart" (2000, p. 221). Research showed that the simple touch of a nurse taking a palpated pulse reading was enough to reduce dangerous arrhythmias in patients with heart problems (p. 232).

"Although touch is an effective healing agent," said one researcher, "it is under-utilized by healing practitioners, from neurologists to social workers, and has been generally ignored by institutions and neglected by researchers" (Field, 1994, p. 16). As medical technologies become more high tech rather than high touch, people will need a place to go for the nurturing comfort of touch that is disappearing in other areas of society. "Laying-on of hands is not merely folklore or mysticism," said another researcher in the same department. "Reinstituting the backrub as standard hospital procedure could balance the introduction of the computerized axial tomography scanner" (p. 17). Spas play an important role in society as a healing institution where the benefits of touch are still cherished and applied.

Energy Work

Some practitioners claim that the healing power of touch comes not so much from the physical manipulation of the tissues in the body, but rather from the facilitating of the flow of energy. Some spa therapies, collectively referred to as "energy work," have evolved to focus more on a healing and nurturing touch than on the deep manipulation of body tissues. An example of this is a technique known as "Therapeutic Touch" (TT) in which the practitioner places their hands on "or slightly above" an injured area to "feel" the problem and "send healing energy" to the site (Newman & Miller, 2006, p. 11). The philosophy of TT is that healing is "a natural human ability" and occurs when there is a "balanced, even flow of energy within a person and between the person and the environment" (Bonadonna, 2002, p. 233). Research is limited on these kinds of spa therapies, although they have been shown to reduce anxiety and "people commonly report feelings of relaxation, lightness, tingling, or heaviness" (p. 235).

Shiatsu, which is commonly found on spa massage menus, is a holistic health care method originating in Japan that is based on using "Oriental energetic diagnosis and body energy techniques to correct imbalances in the body and focuses on the whole person (mind, body, and spirit as an interconnected whole . . .)" (Long, 2008, p. 921). Shiatsu treatment consists of gentle pressure to "energy channels" that are believed to exist along the surface of the body (p. 922). Studies showed that consumers of Shiatsu treatments would try it first "out of curiosity" but repeat clients were seeking "to maintain health" and that they perceived the treatment to be successful in helping them. Clients of an experimental Shiatsu program were found to show reduced medical symptoms and greater uptake of healthy lifestyle behaviors that they attributed to their treatments (Long, 2008).

Reiki is another energy treatment of Japanese origin that is popular in spas. Reiki means "universal (rei) life force energy (ki)" (Honervogt, 1998 as cited in LaTorre, 2005, p. 184). In Reiki, the therapist places their hands over the body but there is no actual massage. If the therapist touches the patient at all, it is very light (Johnson & Redman, 2008). Reiki is said to "rebalance the vibrational field within mind and body although there is no agreed-upon theory on how it works or basic understanding for the mechanism of its actions" (LaTorre, 2005, p. 184). Reiki is thought to be beneficial for clients "who are anxious, stressed, depressed, or in chronic pain (Nield-Anderson & Ameling, 2001 as cited in LaTorre, 2005, p. 185). Reiki has even been suggested as a possible enhancement to traditional psychotherapy treatments since the gentle touch of Reiki can help build a safe relationship between the client and therapist and can model a healthy, calming behavior that clients can consider for reducing stress even when they are at home (LaTorre, 2005).

Another example is craniosacral therapy which is said to be "useful for alleviation of pain from accidents, for stress-related symptoms, for sensory disorders, and to promote overall health" (Wisneski & Andeson, 2005, p. 150). The energy flow being treated in craniosacral is even more literal as this treatment works on releasing the "restrictions in the craniosacral hydraulic system of the body" that are thought to prevent the central nervous system from working properly. The treatment is performed while the therapist gently holds the clients head "'listening' to the rhythms as the body moves" (Johnson & Redman, 2008, p. 222). Craniosacral quite literally works on the connection between the mind and the body.

The mechanisms behind energy treatments are not completely understood but they have shown significant results as a method of reducing anxiety, reducing pain, speeding healing, and for a variety of clinical conditions (Phalen, 1998). It seems that at least some of the results of these kinds of treatments come from helping the patient to relax, and allowing the body's own healing mechanisms to come into play.

The Power of the Mind in Healing

Intention and the Placebo Effect

Intention plays a role in some of the energy work of spa therapies, where it is believed that the "focusing of consciousness" of the therapist directs the energy of the body to facilitate healing (Bonadonna, 2001). Intention is also meaningful to the spa customer because they may begin to see benefits simply from selecting the intention to visit a spa and taking steps for their own wellbeing. The expectation that a customer has when visiting a spa can have a significant impact on the outcome of the experience. One study on using tai chi for stress relief showed the impact of participant expectations. The researchers compared tai chi, walking, meditation and book reading (control group) as different methods for alleviating stress (Jin, 1992). All of these methods were found to help alleviate the stress-response in the participants. Tai chi had a greater calming effect on state anxiety than the book reading, but this effect disappeared when they controlled for the expectations of the participants. In other words, they could not tell if the tai chi was actually more beneficial for relieving stress, or if it was simply attributed to the participants' belief that it would be more beneficial.

The "power of intention" has been popularized by many modern day "self-help" healers such as Wayne Dyer (2004), Deepak Chopra (2003), and Rhonda Byrne in the recent best seller, "The Secret" (2006). But the ability of belief, intention and mental focus to have an impact in reality is not just new age mumbo jumbo. Rather, it is grounded in hard scientific research. In actuality, it may be the *most researched* healing method in all of science: the placebo effect. The placebo effect is a physiological improvement that comes from an "inert" treatment and has been described as "the only treatment common to all societies and cultures . . . its effectiveness has been attested to, without exception, for more than two millennia" (Shapiro & Shapiro, 1997, p. 1).

The effectiveness and persistence of many ancient, alternative and indigenous healing methods (often the staples of a typical spa menu) are commonly attributed to the placebo effect. Some would say that "placebos were the dominant treatment in preliterate cultures" (Shapiro & Shapiro, 1997, p. 3). Belief in magic "played the dominant role in medicine from prehistory well through the Middle Ages" (Kradin, 2008, p.25). Using the "perceived power of the Healer" and other amulets and potions, shamans or medicine men played an exalted role in society (p. 35). These rituals all were useful in creating positive expectations in those who were seeking a cure. Historically, spa-like temples were centers for religious rituals, bathing therapies and other healing treatments "where sick patients were encouraged to partake in activities designed to soothe mind and body" (p. 39). Testimonials from the period suggest that patients responded well to these treatments and spas continue to pay homage to this shamanic healing practice today.

Complementary and alternative medicine practices in general are often attributed to the placebo effect. Some would say that alternative medicine is by default medicine that works primarily by a placebo response. If it was shown to have mechanisms for healing which were scientifically identified in random controlled trials to be effective, it would no longer be considered "alternative" (Kradin, 2008). This doesn't mean that these kinds of healing therapies should be discarded. While "the incredible power of positive placebo responses" has been "undervalued" in American medicine (Phalen, 1998, p. 87), the healing effects of alternative medicines are documented enough to suggest that if they are all attributable to the placebo response, than *all* healers should learn more about how to generate these effects in their patients (Bootzin & Caspi, 2002).

The typical modern example of a placebo is a sugar pill, which has no medicinal value, yet has led to improvements in a vast array of diseases. The placebo effect, while a nuisance for researchers trying to define the impact of active therapies, is not discounted in clinical practice. Most rigorous medical studies are "placebo-controlled," meaning they remove the placebo effect from the data in order to get an accurate measure of the medicine or procedure being studied (Bootzin & Caspi, 2002). But the placebo effect plays a vital role in healing since it describes the body's own healing powers, which have been found in thousands of research studies (Harrington, 2002).

The research on placebo effects has shown that these effects are far from being inconsequential. Researchers use terms like "relatively large" and "robust" to quantify both the size of effects attributed to placebo and the consistency with which such effects are found. In some cases, the placebo effects have even been larger than the effects of the actual medical treatments to which they were compared (Wampold, Imel & Minami, 2007, p. 402). Studies on a variety of symptoms across hundreds of patients found that placebos provided a 35% improvement on average (Beecher, 1955 as cited in Shapiro & Shapiro, 1997). These findings suggest that in some cases, patients could avoid costly and potentially risky health care procedures if they could tap into the mechanisms behind the placebo effect and use it to "augment healing and promote wellness" (Wampold, Imel & Minami, 2007, p. 403). The placebo effect draws upon "the innate ability of the body to heal itself spontaneously" according to the "fundamental biological principle of homeostasis that is believed to exist in all living beings" (Bootzin & Caspi, 2002, p. 125). Sometimes the best treatment is "no treatment" because the simpler treatments do "no harm to patients and let nature heal" (Shapiro & Shapiro, 1997, p. 59).

Norman Cousins, a physician who is well known for promoting the healing power of laughter once said "the history of medicine is the history of the placebo effect" (1979, as cited in Newman & Miller, 2006, p. 132) implying that most effective healing discoveries have come from medicine's ability to enlist people's minds as a healing agent. According to Cousins, "the human body is its own best apothecary" (1995 as cited in Kradin, 2008, p. 12). The very first placebo controlled trial experiment (conducted in 1799) noted "[A]n important lesson in physic is here to be learnt, the wonderful and powerful influence of the passions of the mind upon the state and disorder of the body" (de Craen et al., 1999 as cited in Price, Finnis & Benedetti, 2008).

"Placebo" comes from the Latin verb "placare," which means "to please" (Rajagopal, 2006) and is a name given to any medicine "adopted more to please than to benefit the patient" (attributed to Fox's New Medical Dictionary, 1803 as cited in Shapiro & Shapiro, 1997, p. 29). The paradox of the placebo effect is that if a placebo is by definition, "inert," then there should be no such thing as a "placebo effect." This confusion has plagued medical practitioners for centuries (Price, Finniss, & Benedetti, 2008). In a conference on the placebo effect hosted by the National Institute of Health, they gave the health benefits of these "inert" treatments "new legitimacy" and described them as "real and significant, not make believe; an emperor *with* clothes" (Kleinman, Guess & Wilentz, 2002, p. 1).

The Role of the Mind in Healing

Modern medical practitioners typically try to diagnose and treat the problems of the body without consideration to the beliefs or feelings of the person. Science typically looks at the objective experiences of the world as something completely independent of our subjective feelings (Cahana, 2007). The placebo effect challenges this view of health, however. It is not enough to identify from a Cartesian dualist perspective that the mind and body are distinct and play different roles on each other. Rather, the mind and body are completely integrated as a part of one system, a form of "embodied subjectivity" (Cahana, 2007, p. 2).

Jon Kabat-Zinn, a well-known expert on mindfulness, teaches mindfulness meditation and awareness to medical students (the doctors of the future). He teaches them to ask, "Is there anything else you would like to tell me?" to make sure they are considering the subjective experience of their patients and not only the objective results of an x-ray or lab test (1994, p. 189). Most traditional medical training does not include this kind of education, but Kabat-Zinn feels doctors need to learn how to "listen empathically, treating patients as people rather than solely as disease puzzles" (p. 188). The research on placebo effect has identified the important role that the doctor (and the doctor-patient relationship) has on healing. Much of the future research is geared towards the types of caregiver behaviors that elicit a placebo response. In other words, having therapists who are confident and exhibit expertise and optimism can activate a healing response in their clients, regardless of the therapy being administered (Kradin, 2008).

Mechanisms of the Placebo Effect

To understand the mind's role in healing we should seek to understand the different theories on the mechanisms behind the placebo effect, an area not entirely understood by modern scientists. "Natural remission theory" describes the tendency of many conditions to get better on their own. Any intervention could show a positive impact simply as a function of natural healing occurring over time. This is also an example of "regression to the mean," a phenomenon in which subsequent trials are increasingly likely to move towards the mean (with the mean in most cases being a more healthful state). Another theory is that the placebo effect is a case of "classical (Pavlovian) conditioning." In this theory, patients learn to get better using active medical treatments, but the healing effects are conditioned to occur with a placebo (much in the way that Pavlov's dogs were conditioned to salivate to a bell rather than to actual food; Rajagopal, 2006, p. 185).

These theories do not entirely explain how the placebo effect works, however, because they do not take into account the importance of the patients' expectations and beliefs. Those treatments that are believed by the patient to be more powerful "tend to have a stronger placebo effect" than those that are not (p. 186). For example, placebo injections have a greater effect than oral placebos, presumably because they are perceived as a more serious and powerful intervention by the patient. It now seems that the "simulation of an active therapy within a psychosocial context" is more important than the "inertness" of the placebo agent. The "expectations, desires and emotions of the patient" all play a role (Price, Finniss, & Benedetti, 2008, p. 567).

Some theories suggest that what drives the healing effect is any action "performed by the Healer that imbues the Patient with hope" (Kleinman, Guess & Wilentz, 2002, p. 8). "Generation of hope, a shared belief system, and an emotionally charged, confiding relationship" are the common factors found in healing encounters from a variety of settings and cultures (Frank, 1961 as cited in Shannon, 2002 p. 4). Hope is instilled in a distressed patient when they have a sense that they are in the hands of "an expert clinician" and that they are given an acceptable explanation of their diagnosis and treatment "even if it is a 'myth'" (Bootzin & Caspi, 2002, p. 117). One explanation for the placebo effect is the reduction of stress, which interferes with the body's own ability to heal itself (Kradin, 2008). Creating meaningful settings and treatments make the client feel cared for and give them a sense of control over their own illness and symptoms. Spas have always emphasized the importance of ritual and this ritual of interaction between the healer and patient can instill hope and affect health and wellbeing.

For spas, legitimacy and authenticity in their treatments, which can help generate trust and belief in the healing abilities of spas, can be a self-fulfilling prophecy that can lead to real physiological results for their clients. Spas sometimes do better than other healing institutions at telling the stories and the history behind their treatments. These stories add meaning to the experience that can have a direct impact on the outcome of the treatment. Some have suggested, for example, that the reason chiropractors do better than medical doctors at treating low back pain is not due to the treatment itself, but rather due to an increased sense of meaning and hope given to the patient (Moerman, 2002).

This is not to say that spa treatments are "inert" or do not have real physiological value. But we should not discount the ways the mind can influence healing through the release of endorphins and neurotransmitters that reduce pain and improve nervous system functioning (Rajagopal, 2006, p. 186). Even when real, scientifically validated medical treatments are being administered, their ability to heal or reduce pain is heightened when the treatment is administered in view of the patient, due to the higher expectations of the patient. In studies comparing acupuncture with "sham acupuncture" (where the needle insertions are only simulated or applied too superficially to have a significant effect), it was found that patients' expectations of the results of the treatment, and their belief that they were not in the control group, were more important than whether they had received the active or inert treatment (Price, Finniss, & Benedetti, 2008).

The Mind's Impact on Health

The mind has the ability to affect health positively *and* negatively. The term, "nocebo effect" is used to describe any negative consequences or side effects resulting from an inert placebo. Patients' expectations seem to have a role, whether they believe the medicine will heal them or if they believe it could have some negative side effects (Rajagopal, 2006, p. 187). "Psychosomatic" illnesses (with "psycho" representing the mind, and "somatic" representing the body) are those that are said to be "all in one's head." However many modern medical practitioners now recognize that "virtually every symptom is psychosomatic: a function of the interaction of both mind and body" (Newman & Miller, 2006, p. 10).

The understanding and even embracing of the mind's power in self-healing is becoming more and more accepted across medical fields. In 1993, Larry Dossey, MD, a brilliant internist, published his model of the *Three Eras of Medicine*. In this model, Era I is scientific medicine, focused on observable "facts" and the diagnosis and elimination of symptoms, through suppression or surgery. Era II medicine, as defined by Dossey, is mind-body medicine, with its focus on methods that can help people take an active role in their health. Era III medicine, said Dossey, is transpersonal medicine, focused on methods that bring people to their innate abilities to heal themselves and others (Dossey, 1993, as cited in Newman & Miller, 2006).

Today, physicians recognize the importance of the healing effect of the mind, not only from the standpoint of having to control for it in medical research, but also for the value of the effect itself as an aid for real healing (Wampold, Imel & Minami, 2007). While the mechanisms behind it are still unclear, research has shown that a majority of diseases can be improved simply by the power of the mind believing in the treatment. I am not suggesting that a spa is only a placebo and no other benefit may be gained from it. But spas improve wellbeing in many ways, and one of them is by engaging their customers in a ritual that is performed for their own good. Simply having the right intentions and a place to go to focus on their own wellbeing can have a powerful effect. Spas help people to benefit from the mind's powerful healing properties, even when we don't fully understand them.

The Effect of Time and Mindfulness

A visit to a spa usually consists of a certain amount of time just being in a quiet space, enjoying the experiences one is having or reflecting on whatever is on the mind at the moment. Often the hour that a person spends in a spa treatment is the only hour of waking time they may have being disconnected from technology, disconnected from telephones, and disconnected from the demands of a fast-paced world. Technology has helped us to become so connected, that we have lost the space, and more importantly, the time to disconnect, sit, breathe, relax and reflect.

George Prochnik, the author of *In Pursuit of Silence: Listening for Meaning in a World of Noise* (2010a), writes and speaks about the scarcity of silence "in a world of diminishing natural retreats and amplifying electronic escapes." Spas are one of the last havens of tranquility left in our culture and as Prochnik said, "evidence for the benefits of silence continues to mount" (2010b).

A quiet, tranquil space to escape to can provide the right setting for a meditation practice. Herbert Benson, associate professor of medicine at the Mind/Body Medical Institute at Harvard Medical School, has been a pioneer in research on relaxation. Benson learned "that meditation and other modalities induced beneficial physiological responses. For example, subjects in a meditation group consumed 17% less oxygen, had lower heart and respiratory rates, and had lower blood pressure than did control subjects" (Wisneski & Anderson, 2005, p. 120). Research has found real physiological changes to brain tissues in experienced meditators, particularly in the prefrontal cortex where positive emotions reside (Vaillant, 2008).

Yoga practice also begins with concentration on breathing to quiet the mind. When the mind is quiet, the release of cortisol, our stress hormone, decreases (Kendall-Reed & Reed, 2004). One study of long term yoga practice on women over 45 showed that the more yoga people do, the healthier they are (Moliver, et al., 2011). Researchers and medical practitioners are beginning to recognize relaxation as a critical element to the healing process. Put simply, conventional medicine is more effective on relaxed patients.

Dr. Benson identified the "relaxation response," describing the body's physiological response to relaxation that facilitated healing. He encouraged people to practice slow, deep breathing to elicit this state of relaxation as a part of a healing process he called "wellness remembered"

(Newman & Miller, 2006, p. 48). A lot of the spa's emphasis on stress relief could be attached to the belief that the body's ability to heal itself can be facilitated by simply relaxing the mind and body and allowing them to do their work.

Jon Kabat-Zinn provided meditation training not only for the medical students but also for medical patients because he believed it would help them to stimulate their own self-healing capabilities. The mindfulness-based meditation involves "developing a keen sense of moment-to-moment awareness by observing thoughts and sensations" (Wisneski & Anderson, 2005, p. 120). He found the training was beneficial for patients in reducing pain and anxiety. Kabat-Zinn teaches people to take responsibility for their own health and wellness and not to blindly hand that important job over to the physician/authority figure. Spending time sitting in silence helps people to "listen more carefully" to "the messages from [their] own body and mind and feelings." He calls this "mobilizing the inner resources of the patient for healing" (1994, p. 192).

The most powerful benefits from visiting a spa may come simply from being in a safe space, separated from the interruptions of noise and technology, where a person can become present and tune into the thoughts in his or her own head. Personally, I find I have the greatest flashes of inspiration and insight while I am lying on a massage table. Solutions appear for problems that have been lingering, ideas come without thinking, and stress dissipates into the silence. The scarcity of silence, time and space for reflection in our culture makes these moments sacred. Spas give us that time and space to tap into our spiritual side and reflect on what is important.

Spas also recognize that we live in a high performance society. People are working harder and longer than ever before in the history of humankind. But high performance requires deep moments of relaxation or it cannot be sustained. Simply sitting still for an hour and sipping some tea, or lying quietly in a treatment room while receiving a massage or other treatment, can allow a person's mind to relax and rebalance, so they leave the spa feeling renewed and re-energized.

Reading spa menus today, it is easy to find descriptive statements such as "soothes the mind and the body" or "relaxes you mind, body and spirit." It would be convenient to dismiss this as hyperbole, an exaggerated claim for the sake of marketing the spa. But looking at some of the related research from the field of psychology, we can see that spas do have the power to make good on these claims. The spa does indeed make an impact on mind, body and spirit. Why else do so many keep coming back for more?

CHAPTER 4

Positive Psychology and Spas

Positive Psychology, The Science of Flourishing

The reason I think psychology can play such a meaningful role in the spa and hospitality industries is because ultimately these businesses exist to take care of people. The findings of positive psychology have been summed up with the phrase "other people matter" (Peterson, 2006, p. 249) referencing the importance of relationships and connections with others for human health and happiness. Positive psychology is the study of human excellence and flourishing. It is the study of what is right with people rather than what is wrong with them. That is not to say that traditional psychology is "negative" psychology, but one of the great undertakings of traditional psychology has been the ongoing development of the DSM, the *Diagnostic and Statistical Manual of Mental Disorders* (American Psychiatric Association, 2000). There has been a focus on labeling, classifying, diagnosing and then treating, all of the things that can go wrong with the human mind.

Martin Seligman and Christopher Peterson, two of the founding fathers of positive psychology, felt that it was equally important to develop a classification system for everything that is right with people. They created something that they referred to as the "un-DSM," a *Handbook and Classification of Character Strengths and Virtues* (2004). This text, which is *almost* as comprehensive as the DSM, identifies 24 strengths across six universal categories of virtue: wisdom, courage, humanity, justice, temperance and transcendence. Identifying and fortifying people's strengths is a powerful way to help people live happier, more fulfilling lives (Peterson & Seligman, 2004). People can find their own strengths measurement by visiting www.authentichappiness.com and taking the "VIA" (Values In Action) Survey.

"Happiness" is not necessarily what most spas promote as the desired outcome of their services. But there is certainly some overlap between the concept of holistic wellbeing across mind, body, and spirit and the psychological construct of subjective wellbeing (Diener & Biswas-Diener, 2008). The research I have reviewed seems to indicate the overlap is real and substantial. Consistently, a link is found between happiness or psychological wellbeing and physical health. Satisfaction with life is associated with a higher health-related quality of life, lower rates of chronic illness, and fewer risky health behaviors (such as smoking, drinking and physical inactivity; Strine, Chapman, Balluz, Moriarty, & Mokdad, 2008).

Sheldon Cohen, who won the Positive Health Award at the first annual International Positive Psychology Association World Congress in 2009, has done several studies linking positive emotions to enhanced immunity and reduced symptoms when exposed to a common cold virus (Cohen, Doyle, Skoner, Fireman, Gwaltney & Newsom, 1995; Cohen, Doyle, Turner, Alper & Skoner, 2003; Pressman & Cohen, 2005). Positive affect can get "under the skin" to affect physical health through both biological and behavioral pathways. Biologically, positive emotions are linked to endogenous opioids, which have an effect on autonomic and endocrine activity that affect pain and immune function. Behaviorally, positive emotions are linked to better close personal relationships with partners who are likely to encourage healthy behaviors and discourage risky health behaviors (Pressman & Cohen, 2005).

Happiness has also been linked to longevity, as in the famous "nun study" where researchers analyzed the autobiographies written by 180 young women just as they were entering a religious order. Despite living, eating and working together in very similar conditions, the nuns who expressed the greatest amounts of positive emotions in their writing were more than twice as likely to have outlived those with the least happy autobiographies several decades later (Danner, Snowdon, & Friesen, 2001).

Only recently, researchers have concluded that the relationship between happiness and health is not merely correlational. As one researcher said, "there is growing empirical evidence that positive emotion protects against poor health outcomes in later life" (Ong, 2010). A review of the research done to date has led positive psychologists to conclude that "positive psychological processes are beneficial for health and for neuroendocrine and immune function in particular" (Low, et al. 2011), and more definitively, "happy people live longer" (Diener & Chan, 2011).

Based on this research and much more like it, positive psychologists argue that medical doctors should ask their patients not only about physical health symptoms and behaviors, but also about emotions and happiness (Diener & Biswas-Diener, 2008, pp. 29-30). Objective health and physical wellbeing is inextricably tied to subjective wellbeing and happiness. Spas can use the concepts and language of positive psychology to think about ways to positively impact people in new and meaningful ways. By helping people experience more joy, more pleasure, more fulfillment and greater health, positive psychology is a perfect fit for the world of spas.

The Birth of a New Branch of Psychology

It is important to note that positive psychology is not the same as "self-help" or "happiology." In fact, many of the most prominent researchers in positive psychology have their roots in traditional psychology. Martin Seligman, for example, prior to founding positive psychology, was the president of the American Psychology Association and was well known for his ground breaking research on the concept of "learned helplessness" (Maier & Seligman, 1976). There was nothing "positive" about learned helplessness: he discovered that dogs that were experiencing electric shocks with no ability to control the situation learned that they were helpless. When they were placed in another situation where they could easily escape the shocks, they simply curled up into a ball and whimpered, trapped by their own learned helplessness. This had huge implications for the understanding of the roots of human depression, which has become one of the most widely diagnosed health problems in the world now affecting 15% of the population and predicted to effect 30% by the year 2020 (Murray & Lopez, 1996 as cited in Lyubomirsky, 2007). But the study of learned helplessness led Seligman to ask the question, "Can you also learn optimism?" This inquiry led him on the path towards the positive side of the science (Seligman, 2006).

Likewise, Jonathan Haidt was doing research on "disgust" (research on cockroaches, corpses and feces — not very positive). While he was investigating disgust (for example by discovering that no matter how "sterile" a cockroach was, he couldn't get someone to enjoy eating one; Rozin, Haidt & McCauley, 1993), he also began to wonder what the opposite of disgust was. This led him to develop his theories of "elevation," which is "triggered by witnessing acts of human moral beauty or virtue" (Haidt, 2000, p. 1). Who would have thought that an expert on cockroaches, corpses and feces would become known for his theories on happiness (Haidt, 2006)?

Positive Psychology Is Based on Empirical Research

Another thing that sets positive psychology apart from the "self-help" genre, is that it is based on the scientific method and supported by empirical research using randomized, placebo-controlled trial experiments. To understand the distinction between positive psychology and self-help it may be useful to compare some of the theories that are being presented. One of the most popular self-help books of recent is *The Secret* which promotes the "law of attraction," a way of focusing on the things that you want as a means of getting more of them (Byrne, 2006). This theme has been reflected in self-help books for some time, for example *The Power of Positive Thinking* (Peale, 1966) and *Think and Grow Rich* (Hill, 2007) are two long time bestsellers that both promote the idea that you can create anything that the mind can "conceive and believe" (p. 196).

As it turns out, positive psychology can validate *some* of the findings of these texts. Self-efficacy and self-determination theory, for example, have shown that people's beliefs do have a correlation with their success in achieving outcomes, not because of any magical, mysterious forces in the universe, but rather because these beliefs impact their behaviors, their abilities to cope with challenges, and their relationships with others in their support network (Brown & Ryan, 2004). Furthermore, recent research on positive emotions has shown that positive feelings can be beneficial in ways that were previously not understood. Psychologists have understood for some time the purposes of negative emotions. They prepare us to confront specific problems that we may be facing. Anger and fear prepare us to fight or flee. Sadness and grief help us to withdraw and recompose ourselves after a loss or tragedy. But what do positive emotions do?

Barbara Fredrickson's research on positive emotions has led her to develop the "broaden and build" theory, stating that positive emotions broaden our horizons and make us more open to experiences and stimuli around us, helping us to learn, grow and develop resources over the long term. That openness leads people to develop resources and relationships that can lead to even more positive emotions ("upward spirals"; Fredrickson, 2009, p. 62). Negative emotions solve immediate problems. But positive emotions lead to long term flourishing and growth. Fredrickson identified a three to one ratio of positive to negative emotions that is crucial for human flourishing.

For spa professionals interested in helping their clients to flourish and thrive, this raises the question of how spas can increase people's positivity ratio. Certainly, some of the things spas do obviously fall into this category. Spas provide pleasure, increasing positive emotions, and relieve pain and anxiety, decreasing negative emotions. Spas always want their clients to feel better when they leave than they did when they arrived. While they may not have articulated their goal as increasing the positivity ratio, that is essentially what spas do. Using research from positive psychology can help spas to fulfill this mission.

Applied Positive Psychology

Applied positive psychology is defined as "the application of positive psychology research to the facilitation of optimal functioning" (Linley & Joseph, 2004, p. 4). And since spas are tasked with enhancing the health and quality of life for their patrons (Yaller & Yaller, 1974) and increasing wellbeing through a renewal of mind, body and spirit (ISPA, 2006c), the research and application of positive psychology is a powerful way that spas can achieve their lofty missions. Spas offer treatments, therapies, workshops and classes in order to improve the overall wellbeing and "optimal functioning" of their clients. Positive psychology seeks out and then applies empirically validated methods for improving wellbeing referred to as positive interventions.

Positive psychology is sometimes subject to criticism when the research findings do nothing more than to confirm what has already been identified by the self-help realm or beliefs that have been commonly held and are easily validated by our own intuition. We all want to believe in "The Power of Positive Thinking," but positive psychology seeks to validate these concepts empirically and to understand the mechanisms of how they work.

It is widely accepted, for example, that happy employees are more productive. But the reality is that research on this has not been universally supportive of this idea. The statistical relationship between life satisfaction and work productivity is being looked at closer than ever before and some of the mechanisms of this relationship (optimism [Seligman, 2006], zest [Peterson, Park, Hall & Seligman, in press], intrinsic job satisfaction [Hosie, Sevastos & Cooper, 2006]) are being identified in the research. Likewise, positive psychology can also use research to disprove certain myths which are commonly held to be true. For example, recent research from positive psychology shows us that there is a link between happiness and money, although it may not be as strong as most people tend to believe (Diener & Biswas-Diener, 2008; Di Tella & MacCulloch, 2008).

One of the weaknesses of the spa industry is a lack of scientific research to validate the claims that spas make. Their benefits are supported by the anecdotal evidence provided by their popularity and ubiquitousness across history and culture. But spas could benefit from scientific data, which could be used not only to validate the services they offer, but to educate spa professionals on new and better ways to improve the wellbeing of their customers. The spa industry is now beginning to do some of its own research. The International Spa Association (ISPA) has partnered with Dr. Brent Bauer, an internal medicine specialist of the Mayo Clinic to explore the existing medical research on spa therapies, stress relief and wellness. And thanks to the donations of spa industry leaders like Ruth Stricker of The Marsh and Howard Murad of Murad, the ISPA Foundation has created some small grants to encourage new research in these areas. But the spa industry should also keep an eye on the findings of positive psychology, because research on human excellence and optimal functioning may just lead the spa industry to exactly where it needs to go.

The How of Happiness

Seligman identified a formula for happiness: $H = S + C + V$, which is to say, your happiness (H) is defined by your set point (S), the circumstances in which you live (C), and then there is a certain amount of your happiness that can be influenced by one's own voluntary actions (V) (Seligman, 2002). Another psychologist, Sonja Lyubomirsky, looked at the research to identify *how much* of our happiness is under our voluntary control. She found that 50% of our happiness can be explained by genetics (set point), 10% is explained by your circumstances (government, climate, family setting, etc.). This leaves up to a whopping 40% that may be manipulated by our actions (Lyubomirsky, 2007). I don't take these percentages too literally, but the takeaway for the spa industry is that it is possible for individuals to impact the happiness and the psychological wellbeing of themselves or others, and the science of positive psychology can use randomized placebo-controlled trial experiments to parse out exactly how this can be done.

Now that a handful of psychology researchers that have found their way to this brighter side of life, the question for the spa industry becomes, "What are they learning?" and, "How can we apply it to our own lives *and* our business?" Much of the research has centered on the *how* of happiness—how can people get more of it into our lives? Seligman, for example, identified three pathways to happiness: *the pleasant life*, which is about increasing pleasure, enjoyment and positive emotions; *the engaged life*, which is about increasing engagement and flow; and *the meaningful life*, which is about creating a greater sense of purpose and meaning in one's life (Seligman, 2002). I think spas can have an impact across all three of these pillars. They certainly create pleasure for people; certain spa activities can create a sense of engagement or flow; and when people use spas to either connect with others, reflect on personal values, or to focus on improving their own health, a great deal of meaning can be found.

Spas and the Good Life

The spa industry often wrestles with its own identity. Is a spa a place for healing and wellbeing? For pampering and pleasure? Or is it both? The reality is consumers go to spas for many different reasons: sometimes to address a serious health concern and other times to pass an enjoyable afternoon. Industry research has suggested that people go to spas first and foremost to "reduce stress" and then for "overall wellbeing" (ISPA, 2006a). What does a spa do to enhance wellbeing across mind, body and spirit and how does this fit into the context of the good life as laid out by positive psychologists? Do spas enhance physical health, or are they more impactful on the psychological constructs of pleasure, engagement, and meaning?

Spas and a Life of Pleasure

Scientific support for the actual health benefits of spas is limited and often conflicting, however, people have been visiting spas for thousands of years (Johnson and Redman, 2008). This provides a certain level of evidence that people are receiving some kind of benefit from spa services. There is something about the experience of visiting a spa that contributes to what we think of as "the good life." What is so good about a spa?

"It feels good," is often cited as the reason to go to a spa. This response makes it sound like spas may be bringing happiness in the form of hedonic pleasure more than health. Positive psychologists would argue that feeling good and being well are highly related (Diener & Biswas-Diener, 2008). Research has shown that there are benefits of happiness that go far beyond just feeling good in the moment. In "The Good Life, Broadly and Narrowly Considered," King, Eels & Burton (2004) cited several positive outcomes that happiness predicts, including satisfying relationships (Russell & Wells, 1994), career success (Staw, Sutton, & Pelled, 1994), superior coping (Aspinwall, 1998; Carver, Pozo, Harris & Noriega, 1993), and physical health (e.g., Kubznasky, Sparrow, Vokonas, & Kawachi, 2001). And in "Positivity," Barbara Fredrickson described her "broaden and build" theory that suggests positive emotions bring benefits that go far beyond the feelings themselves. Positive emotions heighten our awareness, open us up to new ideas and inspire us to act on those ideas (Fredrickson, 2009). If spas can play a role in making us feel good, this may have a positive impact across many domains, including health.

Comforts and Pleasures in the Spa World

To understand how spas might contribute to a life of pleasure, consider a distinction between "pleasures" and "comforts." Comforts are "background improvements" to which we readily adapt (Wrzesniewski, Rozin & Bennett, 2003, p. 199). An example of this is air conditioning which starts out by being a pleasant surprise but quickly becomes something that does not warrant our attention until we realize how uncomfortable we are without it. Spas are always designed with comfort in mind, not because the comfort is a meaningful part of the experience, but rather because the absence of comfort would interfere with the pleasure a guest would enjoy. Spas take great pains to create an extremely comfortable environment: guests are provided a soft robe and slippers and the space is designed to provide a sense of privacy in a soundproofed, temperature controlled space with plush furniture designed to encourage relaxation. The comfort of a spa is designed to protect the guests from any distraction that might interfere with their enjoyment of the experience.

The pleasure of a spa experience is what rises above that comfortable backdrop to make a lasting impact on the customer. Pleasures in general are more salient than comforts and are defined as those positive experiences that are "unique events . . . to which we do not adapt" (Wrzesniewski, et al., 2003, p. 199). These are special events that we never become adapted to due to their distinctive and varying nature. Because of this, "it is proposed that pleasures contribute more to the quality of life than do comforts" (p. 199). For most customers, a spa experience is a source of great pleasure, in no small part due to its place as a departure or escape from regular daily life. The uniqueness of the experience, highlighted by a separation from day to day stresses, is a source of pleasure.

Types of Pleasure in the Spa

Psychologists have identified three distinct types of pleasure: sensory pleasure, aesthetic pleasure and the pleasure of accomplishment (Rozin, 1999). Spas have an opportunity to provide pleasure across all three categories, although sensory pleasure is the most apparent since the spa is such a rich sensory environment. While a visit to the spa can stimulate all of the senses, for most people, the sense of touch is the primary source of pleasure from a spa treatment such as a Swedish massage, the typical spa's most popular offering. Touch can be described as being "beneceptive" or beneficial because it can be linked to positive feelings primarily from "contact-comfort" (Rozin, 1999, p. 2).

The sensation of pleasure from touch is unique to our external organs, such as the skin, which has interaction with the outside world. Internally, sensation is primarily used to indicate that "something is wrong" (e.g., aches and pains). The external sense organs, including the skin, are "receptors that line the body/world interface" (Rozin, 1999, p. 2). The fact that they transmit "good news" in the form of pleasure as well as "bad news" in the form of pain may be an indicator of a behavioral/survival mechanism, to draw us towards those things which are good for us. And while people tend to adapt quickly to comforts and some pleasures, "parts of the sensory pleasure system, especially those having to do with pain and some positive skin sensations, show remarkably little hedonic adaptation" (Rozin, 1999). In other words, the spa treatments keep feeling good, no matter how many times you go back for more.

Through a variety of spa treatments, touch is the most significant channel for sensory pleasure, but spas will often reference all five senses in the experience they offer. The spa industry seems to intuitively understand the complexity of pleasure and the importance of incorporating all of the senses into it. One positive psychologist (Peterson, 2006) said that pleasure "is usually compound, simultaneously involving several sensory systems" (p. 48). Spa experiences are usually rich in sensory elements such as delectable menus of spa cuisine, teas and herbal elixirs; fragrant products made with essential oils designed to produce aromatherapeutic benefits; and beautiful music often combined with sounds of nature or trickling waterfalls to induce a state of relaxation.

Combine all of these sensory experiences in a facility which is designed to appeal to the customers' sense of beauty, with lovely artwork, sculptures, water fountains, and soothing, soft lighting, and you can see how spas, in addition to sensory pleasure, also provide "aesthetic pleasure" to their clients. One well known spa designer described her design philosophy as "a healing art," using the aesthetic of the space to create an atmosphere that encourages health and harmony (Clodagh, 2001, p. 14). Her philosophy is that "everything about an environment affects you — the placement of walls, the flow of rooms, the quality of light, the texture of the floor beneath your feet" (p. 15). Spas are often designed with an Asian theme, sometimes using principles of Chinese Feng Shui, which looks at "the relationship between energy and people and their spaces" (p. 39). The beauty of the facility is considered an integral part of the experience and adds to the pleasure that spa customers have while visiting.

The final type of pleasure, and perhaps the least intuitive as a part of the spa experience, is "accomplishment pleasure," defined as "pleasures derived from achieving something of value through mastery" (Rozin, 1999, p. 6). Destination spas, which have the most complete spa offerings, invite their clients to participate in a broad range of activities including fitness classes, yoga, meditation, art, journal writing, etc. It is through these kinds of activities that spa guests experience accomplishment pleasure and learn the satisfaction of achieving "flow" states, when one becomes completely absorbed in the pleasure of the moment (Csziksentmihalyi, 1991).

Going beyond Pleasure: Spas and a Life of Engagement and Meaning

The ideas of "accomplishment pleasure" and achieving "flow" states suggest that spas can impact our satisfaction with life in an even deeper way. Pleasure is obviously something people seek more of, but it is also considered somewhat superficial. This perception gives spas a reputation as being more about fluff than substance. But spas can also offer a level of "enjoyment," which goes beyond pleasure and involves experiences of learning and growth. Spa activities and experiences that are challenging and require people to develop or improve their skills can bring this feeling of enjoyment and engagement. Unlike pleasure, enjoyment comes with an "investment of psychic energy" in an activity that pushes someone to grow or somehow become better than they were before (Csikszentmihalyi, 1990, p. 46).

"Flow" is an example of a pleasurable state where one is completely absorbed in the activity at hand, but the efforts involved to get into this state make it not as preferable as other kinds of simple pleasures which are easier to achieve (Csikszentmihalyi, 1990). People are often attracted, for example, to the idea of relaxing at a spa and being pampered while exerting no effort. They may experience more "flow" or "engagement," however, in a spa that challenges them with activities that push them to learn and to grow. Destination spas often offer extensive flow- inducing activities such as sports (tennis, golf, etc.), art classes, nature walks, or exercise and mind/body classes.

This concept of engagement describes another facet of the broader term, "happiness," which encompasses much more than positive emotions and is a word that is not easily defined. Happiness could be defined as simply the pursuit of hedonic pleasures, in which spas can certainly play a role. But it could also be used to describe a life filled with engagement, meaning and goodness. In his book, *Man's Search for Meaning,* author Victor Frankl argued that while pleasure is important "we are motivated by a will to meaning more than by a will to pleasure" (Ben-Shahar, 2007, p. 43).

Aristotle used the word "eudaimonia" to describe the "good life" in a way that went beyond mere hedonism. He believed that practicing virtue was more important than experiencing pleasure and was the key to a happy and good life (Aristotle, 1962, cited in King, Eells & Burton, in press, p. 6). The differences between pleasure and eudaimonia are subtle, but substantial. Eudaimonia is easily recognized by objective observers, while pleasure is strictly subjective. The folk wisdom of "different strokes for different folks" suggests that what is pleasurable for one may not be for others. But eudaimonistic or virtuous behaviors appear to have more universal foundations, and may require more effort to achieve them (King, et al., p. 6).

The Intrinsic Nature of Spa

Self-Determination Theory (SDT; Deci & Ryan, 1985 cited in King et al., 2004, p. 7) suggests that the most fulfilling aspects of the good life come from pursuing intrinsic rewards: those things that are good in and of themselves. Fulfilling extrinsic desires, such as for material wealth and possessions, is less desirable. Positive psychologists have identified two critical characteristics for activities to enhance the quality of one's life: intrinsic value and fulfillment (Wrzesniewski, Rozin & Bennett, 2003, p. 185). Activities with intrinsic value are those pursued for their own right, and not because of some extrinsic motive.

Spa visits appear, at least to some, to exhibit this tendency. While some people may visit a spa in order to improve health, or reduce stress, for many it is simply an enjoyable way to spend some time. People often see a spa visit as a way to pamper or reward themselves (after achieving a goal or some other accomplishment, for example) and spending time in the spa could be described as "autotelic," meaning an activity "done not with the expectation of some future benefit, but simply because the doing itself is the reward" (Csikszentmihalyi, 1990, p. 67). A visit to the spa can be a nice break from other activities that may be less intrinsic or less fulfilling.

Can the spa experience be described as fulfilling? Fulfilling activities are defined as those that create a "sense of improving the world and the self" (Wrzesniewski, p. 186). Using this definition, spa visits can be extremely fulfilling because they provide spa-goers with a sense that they are doing something good for themselves. Even the gesture of taking time to relax and be pampered can be fulfilling, especially when the person leaves feeling rejuvenated and better able to confront the challenges of daily life.

Earlier I mentioned the role of spirituality in the spa experience and how time at a spa can be used to help people to reflect on their spiritual beliefs or the things in their life that they hold sacred. This is one of the ways that spas can help people to live a life of meaning. There are lots of opportunities for meaning-making within spas. People go to spas to improve their quality of life, to improve their health, or to share in a special experience with a loved one. For that core group of spa-goers that really taps into the spiritual side of the spa experience, they may even feel connected to a higher power during this time.

Pleasure, Engagement, and Meaning: The Full Life

Research has been done to parse out different individuals' orientations to happiness and life satisfaction. Some people value pleasure more, while others may spend more of their energy seeking engagement or meaning. Each of these orientations has been shown to correspond to ratings of life satisfaction. They have also been found to be compatible with each other, so people can pursue happiness in many different ways, all of which can improve life satisfaction (Peterson, Park, & Seligman, 2005).

Spas don't have to be about either pleasure or meaning, but can tap into the synergistic relationship between the two. Yoga is an example of a spa activity that can be enjoyed on many different levels. For some people, yoga simply feels good and is a pleasurable activity. Hatha Yoga, for example, tends to be very relaxing, peaceful and enjoyable and has become one of the most popular yoga styles today. For others, yoga induces a feeling of flow or engagement, by challenging them to learn the various postures and breath control, and pushing their body to go beyond its normal limits of comfort. Ashtanga and Bikram are two yoga styles that are known for being incredibly challenging and giving people that experience of flow. For those who really immerse themselves into the yoga lifestyle, they may find that any yoga style can bring an incredible sense of meaning as they begin to adopt a spiritual practice that brings their mind, body, and spirit into harmony (Csikszentmihalyi, 1990).

Pleasure, engagement, and meaning all overlap and interplay within different individuals to contribute to their overall wellbeing. "When we derive a sense of purpose from what we do, our experience of pleasure is intensified; and taking pleasure in an activity can make our experience of it all the more meaningful" (Ben-Shahar, 2007, p. 44). Spas have an opportunity to leverage this synergy to create healing experiences that are both pleasurable and meaningful.

One expert on meaning, Paul Wong describes many sources of meaning that spas could attempt to provide including "positive emotion, achievement, relationship, intimacy, spirituality, self transcendence, and self acceptance" (Wong, 1998). This is somewhat consistent with Martin Seligman's new vision for the direction of the science of positive psychology towards "flourishing" rather than "happiness."

From Happiness to Flourishing

Seligman now regrets the overemphasis on happiness that he introduced with positive psychology. According to Seligman:

> I used to think that the topic of positive psychology was happiness, that the gold standard for measuring happiness was life satisfaction, and that the goal of positive psychology was to increase life satisfaction. I now think that the topic of positive psychology is well-being, that the gold standard for measuring well-being is flourishing and that the goal of positive psychology is to increase flourishing (2011).

The old theory was too focused on positive emotions, and therefore criticized for being shallow. And positive emotions, engagement and meaning did not exhaust all of the elements that contribute to wellbeing.

In his latest work, Seligman defines flourishing across five elements described by the acronym PERMA:

> Positive Emotions
> Engagement
> Relationships
> Meaning
> Accomplishment (or achievement)

These five things all contribute to human wellbeing, are pursued independently for their own sake, and are each measured independently from the other items on the list. According to Seligman, if positive psychology is to improve human flourishing (and his suggested goal for the field is to have 51% of the world flourishing by the year 2051), then we will have to focus on how to increase PERMA in the world population. If spas hope to increase wellbeing for their customers--helping them to flourish, they will have to think about PERMA too.

Application of Positive Psychology in Spas

Several "positive interventions" are now being studied and some have already been identified in research studies as capable of producing changes (and sometimes *lasting* changes) in human wellbeing. Some of the activities that have proven effective include practicing gratitude by writing a gratitude letter to a close friend or relative, journaling in a positive explanatory style by writing down "three blessings" on a daily basis, or exercising your signature strengths in a new way (Seligman, Steen, Park & Peterson, 2005). I personally have found that growing an awareness of and then exercising your signature strengths can help to increase wellbeing across all five pillars of flourishing: positive emotions, engagement, relationships, meaning and accomplishment.

The word "intervention," also used in conventional medical terms, comes from the latin *inter venire* or "to come between" and is thought of as actions that someone takes (usually an external agent) in order to make a positive impact (usually correcting some kind of problem). A *positive* intervention is distinguished from other types of interventions in a couple of possible ways. First an intervention can be described as positive if it not only makes a positive impact, but it is making that impact in a positive situation i.e., "increasing wellbeing away from zero." A traditional intervention is typically applied in a clinical situation, i.e., to correct some problem. A positive intervention, on the other hand, would be applied to a healthy population to increase their wellbeing even more in a positive direction (J. O. Pawelski, MAPP 602 lecture, September, 7, 2008).

The second way an intervention can be defined as positive is if it is "positive in method." This encompasses interventions performed using positive methods to increase wellbeing by "cultivating pleasant affect, strengths, and/or meaning" (J. O. Pawelski, MAPP 602 lecture, September, 7, 2008). Using and developing strengths in order to overcome a problem or a weakness would be a way of performing an intervention that is positive in method. In this example, it is possible for a positive intervention to be applied even to a clinical population or to resolve a specific problem.

An intervention can be defined as a positive intervention by fulfilling either, or both, of the two qualities mentioned above. It must either be intended to increase wellbeing in those that are already in a neutral or positive state, or it must be intended to increase wellbeing by focusing on the positive aspects of life and living. Regardless of whether a positive intervention is aimed towards a healthy or a clinical population, its goal is to increase wellbeing, which is what makes it so applicable to the world of spas.

The Power of Positive Questions

Positive psychology was created by asking positive rather than negative questions. Rather than asking, "what is wrong with people," it asks, "what about those things that are right" (Peterson & Seligman, 2004, p. 4)? In this way, positive psychology attempts to balance out a longstanding tradition in psychology of focusing on the negative (disease, disorders and depression; Peterson, 2006). Positive psychology has been described as a "refocusing" (p. 18) of the field towards positive areas such as "human goodness and excellence" (p. 5) so that it is "as focused on strength as on weakness, as interested in building the best things in life as in repairing the worst, as concerned with fulfilling the lives of normal people as with healing the wounds of the distressed" (Peterson & Seligman, 2004, p. 4).

This approach of making things better by focusing on the positive has also been developed for application in organizational settings under the name of "Appreciative Inquiry" or "AI." AI is a style of organizational development created by David Cooperrider at Case Western Reserve

University that looks at what is the best in an organization through a process of asking positive questions and using the sharing of stories of the business at its best to co-create a new future (Cooperrider, Whitney & Stavros, 2008). This is a strong departure from the typical deficit-based management approach, which focuses on identifying and solving the problems in the organization.

The spa industry has not escaped the lure of the deficit-based approach. At the upper end of the luxury scale, expectations are high and much of management time is spent on identifying the problems that lead to guest complaints and/or employee turnover. Appreciative Inquiry suggests that spas should shift their attention to what they want more of, and spend more time sharing stories of excellent service and identifying what they do really well (Cooperrider, Whitney & Stavros, 2008).

To a certain extent it is in our nature to want to focus on the negative, resolve all of the complaints, and fix all the problems. Psychologists call this the "negativity bias" (Rozin & Royzman, 2001, p. 296). We see this often in the hotel spa industry because luxury hotels tend to assume that things will go pretty well, and anything that doesn't garners more attention. Hoteliers spend more time talking about problems than they do about goals, pay more attention to guests who complain than those who are happy, and spend more time with lower performing employees than they do with their superstars. Positive psychology does not suggest that businesses should ignore their problems. But recognizing that this negativity bias exists, business managers should at least give equal billing to the positive side of the equation.

This leads to some questions about how this mindset could be applied within the world of spas. Spa managers often discuss the problems and challenges they confront on a day to day basis but how much time do they spend in meetings talking about their goals/dreams/visions of success? Research on positivity in meetings has shown that effective and successful work teams (as measured by objective measures of performance as well as supervisor and colleague ratings) exhibit ratios of almost six positive comments to every negative one in their meetings. Successful work groups had more comments that were positive rather than negative, more inquiry about their associates ideas than advocacy about their own, and more of a focus outwards towards the other members of their team than self-focused (Losada, 1999; Fredrickson, 2009).

Spa employees often find themselves taking care of an unhappy guest, usually by compensating them with refunds, discounts or showering them with amenities in order to get back in their good graces. This can be highly demotivating to employees to invest all of their energies and direct all of their leverage towards the guests who have treated them the worst. How can spas reward the customers who appreciate them? How do they give employees the autonomy to extend a good-will gesture to a guest for no other reason than that they were a pleasure to serve?

In the spas I've directed, I have always given my employees the power to give something away to guests that they really liked. This program has always been a success for me for three different reasons: First, my staff *never* took advantage of this freedom. Actually, they really exercised this option a lot less than I thought they should have. So the costs of what I was proposing were always minimal. Second, when this option was exercised, both the guests who were the recipients *and* the employees who gave things away felt a sense of elevation and what I imagined to be a heightened feeling of loyalty towards the spa. Finally, whether the employees exercised this option or not, they had a greater sense of control and meaning in their jobs, and were better able to reconcile those moments when they did need to give things away to difficult guests to compensate them for problems and complaints.

This is a great way to create a positive interaction between managers and employees. Unfortunately, many managers spend most of their time having negative interactions with their worst employees (Buckingham & Coffman, 1999). How can spas encourage their managers to give equal billing to their best employees to cultivate that relationship and to communicate how much they are valued? One way to do this may be to work on identifying the strengths of the best employees and figuring out ways to help them apply those to their job. This is a concept that can be applied to all employees, but the point is for managers to consider ways to increase the number of positive interactions with low performing employees and to increase the number of interactions in general with high performing employees.

Positive Questions and Spa Guest Experience

Positive questions can also be used to enhance or increase awareness of the guests' positive experience in the spa. Typically, at the end of a spa treatment, a spa associate will ask, "How was everything?" This is a seemingly neutral question (neither positive nor negative) unless you consider that this question is regularly asked by a variety of businesses as a way of determining if there were any problems that need to be addressed before the customer departs. A positive version of the question would be, "What was the best part of your experience?" or "What would you like to remember about today?" These kinds of questions help the guest to savor their experience, develop more positive emotions, and enhance the bond with the person they are sharing their positive experiences with (Gable, Reis, Impett & Asher, 2004), and since research suggests that the ending of the experience is most important to how the guest recalls it, cueing them to think of the best part at the end could help to enhance the psychological impact of the experience (Kahnemann, 1999).

Peak-end Theory

Daniel Kahneman, a Nobel Prize winning psychologist, established peak-end theory, showing that people tend to remember events based on the peak and end moments more than any other part (1999). Some of the studies were done on colonoscopy patients who were asked to rate the level of pain over the course of their colonoscopy procedure. Regardless of the duration of the exam, the patients who endured a lot of pain in the last minute were more likely to describe the experience negatively, and less likely to return for their follow-up exam a year later. They even showed that doctors could extend the treatment by adding an extra 30 seconds of "less painful" time with the scope in, and increase the patients' likelihood of returning for their follow up appointments. This is ironic since, even though the patient experienced "less pain" for the last 30 seconds, objectively a shorter colonoscopy should have less total pain and discomfort than an extended one.

This research, and others like it, has shown that people tend to have "duration neglect" when remembering past experiences. Kahneman called this "evaluation by moments" meaning people are likely to remember specific moments that are later reconstructed to define in a person's memory their experience (Kahneman, 1999, p. 20). Whether an experience is good or bad, the duration does not appear to be calculated in our remembrance of the event. What are salient in our memories are the peak moments and the end moments, and so these are the moments that have the most psychological impact.

Also, customers often look forward to their spa visits with great anticipation and then afterwards, enjoy the moments when they can reflect back on it and/or share the story with others. Pleasures are often considered to have a greater effect on life satisfaction because the length of enjoyment is extended to include the anticipation of the event before and the memory of it afterward (Wrzesniewski, et al., 2003, p. 199). Because memory of the experience is an large part of its overall enjoyment, it is a good idea for spa providers to consider how elements of a spa visit will be remembered afterwards. Kahneman's "peak-end rule" (2000) predicts that spa customers will neglect the duration in their assessment of a prior spa experience and will instead evaluate it based on the peak of the experience and how it ended. Professionals in the spa industry should take great care in planning how their experiences will end. Aggressive post-treatment sales tactics or a lengthy, stressful check-out process can subtract from the memory of the positive experience of the treatment itself.

Spas typically spend more time thinking about the "sense of arrival" in the way a spa's facilities and services are designed than they do thinking about how the experience ends. Spas may be able to improve the psychological impact of their treatments by crafting great endings to each treatment (saving the best of the treatment for the end or adding a unique value-add to the end of the treatment) and by creating departure rituals so that the customer leaves in the best possible state.

Paradox of Choice

Another one of the most interesting findings of positive psychology is the fact that in spite of objective improvements on virtually every aspect of life over the last 50 years (increased wealth, technology, infrastructure, convenience, choices, etc.) people are not measurably happier (Diener, 2000 as cited in Schwartz & Ward, 2004). Not only are people not happier, but depression is at an all-time high (Lyubomirsky, 2007) and is affecting people at younger and younger ages (Reivich & Shatte, 2002). Some have suggested that although having more choices is universally valued as an indicator of increasing freedom and autonomy, this can have a negative effect on our subjective wellbeing. It is possible to "do better, but feel worse" (Schwartz & Ward, 2004).

This is of importance for the spa industry because spas have the assumption that one way to increase benefit to their customers is to give their guests more options. Spas offer their guests a variety of treatments, activities, facilities and menu items. Logically, it would seem that giving guests more options can only improve their experience. For example, adding more types of massage to the spa menu could provide a better option for someone who could not find what they were looking for on the original list. But for anyone whose favorite massage was already on the original list, they could simply ignore the new options and still be equally happy. . . or can they?

Giving people too many options makes it more stressful for them to make a decision (Schwartz, 2004). Considering the spas' role in stress-relief, this is the last thing that a spa would want to do to their customers. But spa menus have grown substantially over the years. What used to be rare or unique services such as hot stone massage, reflexology, or Thai massage are now staples, adding more options and complexity to typical spa menus. And spas continue to add new and interesting treatments to their menus in order to set themselves apart from their competition.

The studies on choice show that not only does having more options make the decision making process more stressful, but it also means that the person will be less satisfied with the choice they eventually select. From an economist's perspective, the "opportunity cost" of any choice is the loss of the second choice option and that should be weighed into any decision. But what actually happens, is the mind tends to compare the final selection to a combination of all the best features of the bypassed choices, causing them to regret what they ended up with (Schwartz & Ward, 2004, p. 95).

For example a spa guest may be trying to choose between a relaxing Swedish massage, an invigorating body scrub, and a Thai massage to stretch out sore or tight muscles. Once they have compared all three of these options, it will be hard for them to be satisfied unless they can find a treatment which is simultaneously relaxing, invigorating and involves stretching of the muscles. Some spas have found a solution to this problem by offering completely customized experiences. The guest simply books time in the spa and once the guest arrives, the therapist and the guest create a custom spa journey that is designed to exactly meet the needs of that particular guest. This can be a good option, especially if the therapist is skilled at recommending things to the guest or guiding them so they do not feel the stress of having to decide exactly how the whole treatment should go themselves.

For other spas, the message is clear. The spa menus should be simplified as much as possible, perhaps categorized by the intended outcome of the treatment with only one or two treatments available to meet each guest need. Simplified spa menus may not be as appealing to the small percentage of "core" spa-goers who "experiment more when at spas and expect a broader array of 'authentic,' indigenous as well as health and wellness oriented services" (ISPA, 2004, p. 5), but they could help the vast majority of spa-goers that are not in this category to have less stress while selecting their spa experience, and to be more free to enjoy the experience they ultimately end up with.

Gratitude

Many of the most powerful empirical results from studies on positive interventions have involved gratitude in some way. Expressing gratitude seems to be a sure-fire way for someone to enhance their own happiness and wellbeing. Improvements in wellbeing have been found in studies where participants are asked to write down "three blessings" or three things that they are thankful for on a daily basis, or are asked to write a letter of gratitude and deliver it in person to someone deserving (Seligman, Steen, Park & Peterson, 2005). In other studies, journaling about gratitude was shown to be associated with more exercise, fewer physical health systems, higher optimism and positive feelings, and many other positive outcomes (Emmons & Crumpler, 2000; Emmons & McCullough, 2003 as cited in Peterson & Seligman, 2006).

From among the 24 strengths that Peterson and Seligman have classified in their *Handbook and Classification of Character Strengths and Virtues*, gratitude is one of five strengths that had a significant correlation with life satisfaction (the others are hope, optimism, zest and love; Park, Peterson, & Seligman, 2004). In *The How of Happiness,* Sonja Lyubomirsky listed several ways that gratitude increases happiness: it promotes savoring of enjoyable events, bolsters self-esteem, helps people to cope with stress and trauma, and melts away negative emotions (2007). Not only are they happier, but Peterson & Seligman suggested that "grateful people might actually live longer than the nongrateful" (2004, p. 563) citing research that linked longevity with expressions of gratitude and other positive emotions in early-life autobiographies (Danner, Snowdon, & Friesen, 2001).

On a typical spa visit, people have a substantial amount of time in silence for personal reflection before, during and after their treatments. Spas could help their clients if they can encourage them to use some of this time reflecting on what they most appreciate. Robert Emmons, the editor in chief of the *Journal of Positive Psychology* and the field's leading expert on gratitude, suggested a practice of "breathing gratitude" that could be easily incorporated into a spa experience. He cited an exercise known as the "Breath of Thanks" that involves simply taking deep, mindful breaths while repeating the words "thank you." This exercise is intended to "remind yourself of the gift of your breath and how lucky you are to be alive" (Luskin, 2002 as cited in Emmons, 2007, p. 198).

From my experience, many spa customers are brought to the spa as a gift from someone else, so they already have much to be thankful for. When the spa makes the experience enjoyable, they help their client even more because "the more the receiver values the gift, the more likely they are to experience gratitude" (Emmons, 2007, p. 37). Spas should also teach their employees, who are regularly scripted to say "thank you" to their customers, to understand the importance of feeling and expressing true gratitude for every person that comes in the door. The benefits of gratitude disappear when it is forced or inauthentic, but encouraging a culture of gratitude can allow people to develop a practice of appreciation that is natural and intrinsically motivated.

CHAPTER 5

Spas and Stress

The culture of spa is about creating a "spa lifestyle" based on balance and holistic health (Johnson & Redman, 2008, p. 8). As mentioned previously, the true benefit of a spa visit comes when someone learns skills and behaviors and adopts them into their lifestyle to change long-term health and wellbeing. Many of the services offered in the spa are meant to be incorporated into the clients' lifestyle for long after their visit to the spa is over. Fitness and exercise, healthy eating, proper skin care and grooming, and mind-body practices that contribute to greater relaxation and mindfulness are all examples of activities offered in spas that are designed to be part of an ongoing healthy lifestyle.

A Primer on Stress

One of the main lifestyle factors that bring people into spas is *stress.* More and more people are seeking techniques, lifestyle modifications, or places to go to escape from stress. Psychologist Robert Epstein said that 25% of our happiness is determined by our ability to manage stress (Pelaez, 2011). And spa goers cite "reduce stress" as the number one reason they go to spas (over "overall wellness" or "improve my appearance"). The more avid a spa-goer the consumer is, the more likely they are to cite stress reduction as their primary reason to visit spas (ISPA, 2006a).

Many spa-goers describe the spa as an "escape" or haven (ISPA, 2006a, p. ix). It is a place where people can go to not only get away from the stresses of daily life, but to take a moment to gather themselves, to have quiet reflection and practice relaxation in a safe environment. Studies on the consumer spa experience have emphasized the need for the spa environment "to be fully guided and psychosocially safe" so that people can feel protected from the stress and anxiety that they normally encounter. Because spa consumers have stress on the mind when they go to the spa, it makes sense for the owners, operators and employees of spas to understand the basic science behind stress, and to be better educated in how their services and offerings might be able to alleviate it.

The Good Side of Stress

Stress is not necessarily a bad thing. Although stress has been demonized in our culture, what we experience as stress is an important biological process designed to prepare our bodies to confront whatever challenges they may have before them. Stress is the great motivator that keeps us striving for better conditions and a better life. Without stress, we might not be pushed to work as hard as we do to improve our own life and the society around us (Reivich & Shatte, 2002).

Almost every advancement ever made in our civilization could be linked in some way to the avoidance of stress as its primary motivator. To avoid the stress of the elements we have developed comfortable clothing and climate-controlled environments to allow us to live comfortably in any season or locale. To avoid the stress of conflict with nature and with others we have developed complex societies with structures and systems to protect us from harm. To avoid the stress of wanting, we have developed systems of wealth and we strive every day for a better life. If we did not feel stress, we would contentedly lie about while we froze, starved to death, or are killed by someone or something else. The point is, stress has a purpose.

When we are confronted with a challenge or danger, our bodies activate a stress-response to prepare us to handle the situation before us. Energy is rapidly mobilized within the body, sending glucose and other nutrients to the muscles to be used for fight or flight. Energy storage is inhibited so that all energy in the system is available for use. Other long term uses of energy are curtailed, such as tissue repair, sex drive, ovulation, etc. The immunity system, which is normally focused on protecting us from long term health threats, is also inhibited so that the body's energy can focus on the challenges at hand. Pain becomes dulled, so the mind and body can withstand any trauma that occurs during the stressful encounter, and cognitive functions sharpen and narrow so we can maximize our ability to resolve the immediate problem before us (Sapolsky, 2004, p. 11-12).

While it is easy to understand the physical challenges from an evolutionary standpoint—an animal is attacked in the wild and stress levels rise while they confront their aggressor; or tribes are forced to relocate as drought conditions have left their soil unsuitable for agriculture — most humans in the modern world experience a great deal of stress in spite of the fact that we do not live under constant fear of predators, drought or plague.

Robert M. Sapolsky, professor of biology and neurology at Stanford University, described three types of challenges that create stressful conditions for human beings (and all animals for that matter). First are "acute physical crises," which include being attacked, being injured, or other sudden traumatic experiences. "Chronic physical crises" describe more sustained challenges such as food and water shortages and problems with the environment. And finally, and perhaps most importantly for modern-day human beings, "psychological and social disruptions," which can occur any time there is a break down in the relationships and/or communication with those closest to us (2004, p. 4).

The stress that most people experience today has much less to do with a fear of physical threats or scarcities. Most of it boils down to our own emotional reactions to the relationships and experiences we have, more often than not while at work. Challenges in the workplace both real and imagined test our stress response on a regular basis. Often times it is not the situation itself, but how we react emotionally to it that puts us into a stressful state (Reivich & Shatte, 2002). Because we spend much of our waking hours at work, job satisfaction is strongly associated with our mental and psychological health, and job burnout can be a leading cause of stress (Faragher, Cass & Cooper, 2005 as cited in Hosie, Sevastros & Cooper, 2006).

Stress and the Mind

The stress response not only releases hormones that help us to fight or flee in the midst of physical threats, they also release hormones that help us to "tend and befriend" to strengthen us socially and psychologically (Sapolsky, p. 33). Even from an evolutionary perspective, caring for one's family and building strong social ties is an important response to challenge and confrontation. Today, people experience stress while jockeying for position with co-workers while trying to advance their careers, or making big life-changing decisions such as buying a home or starting a family. The way we respond to adversity has a lot to do with our psychological reaction to the situation. People are more resilient to stress when they feel they have a sense of control over their surroundings, they are engaged in their work, and they view change as an opportunity for growth and not as a stressor (Reivich & Shatte, 2002). Having coping strategies, outlets to express frustration, supportive relationships, and a sense that things are getting better are all psychological resources that can help to reduce stress (Wisneski & Anderson, 2005).

Sapolsky's book, *Why Zebras Don't Get Ulcers*, used the analogy of zebras because they use the stress response as it was designed to be used (2004). It protects them from harm, mobilizes them to flee from a dangerous situation, and then it simply lets go. The body returns to normal, stress hormones are flushed from the system, and the body returns to activating its immunity systems, reproductive systems, and energy storage systems that are meant to be in operation during non-stressful times. Most of what occurs in the stress response is not actually negative, but rather is designed to help our bodies confront or flee from dangerous situations, dedicate energy to what is most necessary for survival, and sharpen our thinking so we can quickly solve problems.

The challenge with humans is we seem to have a hard time "letting go" and so we hold onto stress, ruminating on problems long after they are over, and anticipating problems that we haven't even confronted yet. Research has shown that people can be taught psychological strategies to lessen their stress reactions to adverse situations by telling them to stay detached from the situation and by telling them to employ strategies to distract themselves from the stressors that are present. The strength of self-regulation, which we will discuss in detail in the next chapter, can play a role in helping people to control their attention and response to the adversity around them (Mischel, 2004).

The Science of Stress

Stress in and of itself is not bad, but the chronic state of being in stress response has some serious health implications. The health problems from chronic stress were first identified serendipitously by Hans Selye in the 1930s (1979, as cited in Sapolsky, 2004, pp. 7-8). He was attempting to measure the effects of ovarian extract injections on lab rats and found instead that the stress of being caged, mishandled and injected every day was causing peptic ulcers in his research subjects. Selye was the first to identify the stress response and found that the rats' adaptation to anxiety was consistent regardless of the cause of the stress. He also found that there were serious health consequences to adapting to stressors on an ongoing basis.

Selye called the body's "nonspecific response" to stress the "general adaptation syndrome" now known as "the stress response" (Wisneski & Anderson, 2005, p. 76). It is the body's attempt to maintain a state of balance or homeostasis in a constantly changing environment. The stress response has been defined as "the body's constant effort to right any physical or mental stressor, maintaining physiological, mental, and emotional harmony or homeostasis" (p. 77). This state of harmony is called "allostasis" or the ability of the body to "achieve stability through change" (McEwen, 1998 as cited in Wisneski & Anderson, 2005, p. 83). When we are unable to attain this state of harmony, the body's physiological responses places an "allostatic load" on the systems. We experience this as stress, which motivates us to change the situation to alleviate the feeling of anxiety. When we go too long without being able to achieve balance, the body enters into a disease state.

Selye's research went so far as to identify this as a hormonal reaction that involved the hypothalamus, pituitary and adrenal glands. Over time, he discovered the relationship between glucocorticoids and the body's inflammation response and how this played a role in linking stress to disease. And finally, he uncovered what is now widely known today, that the adrenocorticotropic hormone (ACTH) and cortisol, both involved in the adaptation response, can influence health and immunity (Wisneski & Anderson, 2005).

Cortisol is released during stressful situations to mobilize fuel in the body for increased energy, increased immunity, heightened memory function, and reduced pain sensitivity, basically preparing the body to fight or flee whatever challenge it is confronting. Selye found that cortisol and other glucocorticoids, in small doses, were beneficial and actually enhanced the body's immune system. This kind of "low grade stress" was not only physiologically beneficial but could even be "pleasantly stimulating" (Wisneski & Anderson, 2005, p. 78).

Occasional bouts of stress energizes certain systems of the body, ultimately strengthening it and preparing it for whatever challenges may lay ahead. Some have described acute stress as "the body's way of staying in shape" (Wisneski & Anderson, 2006, p. 84) to be prepared to overcome challenges. The stress response in some ways is like a muscle and must be exercised occasionally so that it can perform optimally when it is needed.

Excess cortisol, however, over prolonged periods of time can have a negative impact that outweighs the short term benefits. For this reason, chronic stress leads to impaired cognitive functioning, blood sugar imbalances, higher blood pressure, and increased abdominal fat, all of which are factors in many kinds of bad health problems including hypertension, cardiovascular disease, increased risk of stroke, and reduced immune system (R. Fowler, MAPP 700 lecture, November 15, 2008).

Interestingly, most absences from work and most visits to primary care physicians are due to stress-related illnesses (Kendall-Reed & Reed, 2004).

Because people today live longer than they did 100 years ago, the ravages of stress have more time to wreak havoc on the human body. Medical doctors identify chronic stress as "the root of much of our woe, both physiologically and psychologically" (Ratey & Hagerman, 2008, p. 77). Stress is said to accelerate the aging process, since reduced defenses to disease, slower wound healing, increased likelihood of cancer, and decreased levels of hormones in the blood stream are all signs of aging that are aggravated by stress (Wisneski & Anderson, 2005, p. 97). It is no wonder that stress relief and anti-aging are side by side as two of the common themes that run through spas' diverse offerings.

When Good Stress Goes Bad

Stress can be good, motivating us and helping us to learn, adapt and grow to overcome the challenges we confront in our surroundings. But once the stress level gets notched up past a certain point, or becomes a chronic part of our lifestyle, it can be bad, wreaking havoc on our immune systems and over time having adverse effects on our health. How do we know when good stress goes bad?

The negative aspects of stress are covered by the term "distress" referring to the feelings of inadequacy, insecurity, helplessness or desperation that we experience when the pressure gets too high (Selye, 1974 as cited in Hosie, Sevastos & Cooper, 2006). Far lesser known, is the term "eustress," used to define the beneficial levels of stress associated with motivation and achievement. While people do not want to be in a state of distress all the time, they also do not want to be in a situation where they are not challenged at all. A complete lack of stress leads to complacency and boredom. In our culture, we tend to think of stress as only bad, and that the more stress that we have the worse off we will be.

In actuality, stress can be considered to live on a continuum. Extremely low levels of stress ("hypostress") are unhealthy because they cause us to "rust out" feeling unchallenged and underachieving (Forster, 2005 as cited in Hosie, Sevastros & Cooper, 2006, p. 19). When we become challenged sufficiently, we experience "eustress," which motivates us to learn and grow and be the best that we can be.

Positive psychologists have defined optimal experience, not as moments of passive stress-free relaxation, but as moments of full engagement, when we feel challenged and are applying voluntary effort towards worthy pursuits. This state of "flow" that I mentioned previously occurs when the level of stress or challenge is sufficiently balanced with our skills and capabilities to meet that challenge (Csikszentmihalyi, 1990).

When the challenge gets too great, we fall into "distress" feeling anxiety and nervousness and risking long-term health consequences. Finally, we reach "hyperstress" when the stress level becomes almost unbearable and we experience "burnout" (Forster, 2005 as cited in Hosie, Sevastros & Cooper, 2006).

One way that spas can help their clients is by giving them the knowledge and education to identify the healthy aspects of the stress they may be feeling. People's own lack of understanding about their own reactions to stressful situations can magnify the stress response and cause more of a negative health impact. By viewing their own stress response more clearly and more positively, people can manage their stress in a healthier way (Barbieri, 1996). Since much of stress is created by people's psychological reactions to things, teaching them to have a more positive response to the stressors in their life can keep them from sliding out of eustress and into distress.

Spas and Stress Relief

Negative stress occurs when a person is unable to find a reasonable allostatic balance between not enough and too much of the stress response. For a spa to adequately help their clients address this issue, they need to offer ways to help them maintain balance in the face of adversity. The key is to produce the right conditions for balance between the sympathetic portion of the autonomic nervous system that responds to stress and the parasympathetic portion that facilitates relaxation (Wisneski & Anderson, 2005).

Spa Treatments for Stress Relief

Massage, which is the most popular service offered at spas (Johnson & Redman, 2008,) is beneficial to the autonomic nervous system and may help to reduce pain, support the immune system and relieve anxiety. Some body work techniques, such as "rolfing" or the "Trager method" are said to use manipulation of body tissue as a way to facilitate the release of deep emotions that can be contributing to the stress response. Others, such as "craniosacral therapy" are gentler, where a light touch of the therapist's hands is said to help energy flow and create a soothing experience that relieves stress-related symptoms (Wisneski & Anderson, 2005).

Massage has been shown to increase naturally calming and pain-killing hormones, such as enkephalins and endorphins, while simultaneously decreasing the levels of stress hormones like cortisol in the body. In one study, 52 patients that had been hospitalized for anxiety and depression were given 30 minute daily massages for 5 days in a row. At the end of just one week, the experimental group had lower levels of stress hormone in the blood, urine and saliva, and greater subjective reports of reduced anxiety compared to a control group (Kendall-Reed & Reed, 2004).

Many of the stress relieving benefits of massage therapy are associated with the body's relaxation response. But massage also improves circulation which helps to increase the functioning of the immune system. By improving blood flow to all areas of the body, massage helps to deliver stress relieving nutrients that promote healing to different areas of the body while simultaneously removing the inflammatory by-products that can hinder it (Kendall-Reed & Reed, 2004).

A new research study from The Journal of Alternative and Complementary Medicine entitled "A Preliminary Study of the Effects of a Single Session of Swedish Massage on Hypothalamic-Pituitary-Adrenal and Immune Function in Normal Individuals" compared two groups of healthy adults, one of which received a Swedish massage, while a second control group received a "light touch" treatment. They found some significant positive differences in the group experiencing the Swedish massage particularly with respect to Arginine Vasopressin (AVP), a hormone thought to play a role in stress and aggression. Smaller but significant effects were found in an increased quantity of lymphocytes in the blood (related to immunity) and cortisol hormones (related to stress.)

This research is important because it is a rare example of massage research done on a healthy population (representative of most spa-goers). Most research on massage has been done on clinical populations (e.g., cancer patients, surgery patients, etc.) and "although these studies suggest that massage therapy may benefit certain individuals . . . methodological problems in studies of massage severely limit their ability to generate scientifically valid and generalizable conclusions" (Rapaport, Schettler & Bresee, 2010). This is especially relevant for the spa industry, which (for the most part) caters to healthy consumers and markets its services as preventative and beneficial to the general public, not as a treatment for specific ailments.

This study also showed benefits even against a light touch control group. So although I argued previously that much of the benefits of massage could be attributed to the effects of the touch of a nurturing therapist, this research shows that the massage therapy techniques may also have significant value. While avid spa-goers can speak anecdotally about the benefits of massage, there are so many confounding things happening in the experience that it is hard to say how much impact the massage itself had. But in this study, the control group experienced all of those confounding elements so only the technique of how the massage was applied was different. (The experimental group received typical Swedish massage techniques including "effleurage, petrissage, kneading, tapotement, and thumb friction." The control group received "only a light touch with the back of the hand"; Rapaport, Schettler & Bresee, 2010).

The other thing that makes this particular research study so interesting is that they found this benefit in only a single session of massage. It is easy to imagine that a lifestyle that includes regular massage and relaxation would lead to less stress and greater health. What was surprising to the researchers was that they could see an effect even after a single treatment. This *is* surprising, because even though we in the spa industry believe in what we have to offer, we also know that guests have to come in regularly and shouldn't expect a miracle to happen in a single visit. But this study was able to conclude "that a single session of Swedish massage may have fairly profound acute effects on the immune system" (Rapaport, Schettler & Bresee, 2010).

Although there is much to celebrate here, even in the spa industry we have to take these findings with a grain of salt. Nothing is "proven" by a single research study. But a study like this that finds a stress relieving effect on a healthy population after a single session opens the door for further research. Just by uncovering that there is something here that is measurable, it invites other scientists to dig deeper. And in digging deeper, we just may discover there is much more to spa than most people realize.

The Relaxation Response in the Spa Setting

Aromatherapy oils used in the spa (Amber, Bergamot, Camphor, Cedarwood, Lavender, Poppy and Ylang-ylang, in particular) are also said to aid in stress relief (Kendall-Reed & Reed, 2004). There is very little literature on the mechanisms behind aromatherapeutic healing techniques. More research should be done to determine both the physiological and psychological impact (if any) of using different aromas to effect healing and relaxation. But aromatherapy appears to be one of the fastest growing modalities in the field of complementary alternative medicine (d'Angelo, 2002). And the popularity of aromatherapy treatments and product sales suggests that there is something about these different scents that has a perceived soothing effect that appeals to spa consumers.

Spa therapists can incorporate other stress relieving exercises into their treatments to help their clients learn how to stay calm. Some experts, for example, recommend "positive imagery" or "progressive muscle relaxation" as techniques for helping people to relax and release anxiety (Reivich & Shatte, 2002). In positive imagery, the client would visualize a soothing and calming scene that could be recalled any time they felt themselves reacting to a stressor in a negative way. Progressive muscle relaxation entails tightening, and then relaxing, all the muscles of the body, one area at a time. By learning and practicing these kinds of exercises, a spa consumer could develop techniques that can be employed to stay calm in stressful situations, or to return to a calm state once stressed.

Some of the stress-relieving aspects of the spa have simply to do with being in a relaxing and soothing environment. For example, spas typically serve a cup of hot tea before and/or after treatments and tea drinking has been shown to positively impact both subjective levels of stress and relaxation as well as biological measures of cortisol and platelet activation (Steptoe, Gibson, Vuononvirta, Williams, Hamer, Rycroft, Erusalmsky & Wardle, 2006). Even the music played during spa treatments can have a positive effect since research has shown that "relaxation-inducing activities such as listening to music" can reduce anxiety in extremely stressful situations (Miller, 1979; Affleck, Urrows, Tennen, & Higgins, 1992; Taylor & Brown, 1988, as cited in Mischel, 2004, p. 117).

Mind-body Exercises

Mind-body training often offered at spas can also be beneficial for stress relief. Mindfulness meditation, characterized by "developing a keen sense of moment-to-moment awareness by observing thoughts and sensations" has been shown to be beneficial for patients with both chronic pain and anxiety disorder (Wisneski & Anderson, 2005, p. 120). By training spa clients' minds to observe their reactions, spas can help them to "mitigate [their] reactions to stress" (p. 137). Mindfulness training helps people to observe their thoughts in a non-reactive way, avoiding the reactions that lead to a harmful stress response.

The benefit of practicing this kind of meditation "is that it can literally sever the link between negative thoughts and negative emotions" (Fredrickson, 2009, p. 167). People who practice these skills can avoid having a stress response to stressful situations and develop the ability to induce a relaxation response at will. Research has shown that experienced meditators and first-timers alike had better responses to a stressful situation than a control group that was told simply "to relax." So something about meditation seems to be beneficial across both subjective and physiological measures of relaxation, and the effects seem to get stronger in experienced meditators (Goleman & Schwartz, 1976).

Researchers have identified four components of mindfulness training that appear to have a role in stress reduction: 1) attention regulation: gives people greater control over where they focus their attention; 2) body awareness: so they listen and respond to the natural cues their own body gives them; 3) emotion regulation: so they experience, benefit and learn from their emotions without being controlled by them or carried away by them; and 4) sense of self: so they know who they are and what they stand for (Holzel, et al., 2011).

The awareness developed by mindfulness practices helps people to recognize their own responses to the situations around them. Mindfulness usually involves an acceptance of the present moment, as if the individual is more of an observer than a participant and can let go of any attachments to specific desires that ultimately cause feelings of stress. Since much of stress comes from our own judgments about the situations we are experiencing, practicing "non-judgmental" awareness can help people to learn how to experience things without having an adverse "stressed out" reaction (Barbieri, 1996, p. 10).

Because most westerners are unaccustomed to meditation practices, some mindfulness experts suggest using mind-body exercises as a way of using movement to help the individual stay in the moment (Barbieri, 1996). Meditation (Wisneski & Anderson, 2005), and other mind-body exercises such as yoga (Kendall-Reed & Reed, 2004; Jin, 1992; Barbieri, 1996), tai chi (Jin, 1992; Barbieri, 1996), walking meditation (Barbieri, 1996), Pilates, or martial arts (Charlesworth & Nathan, 2004) that encourage the practitioner to slow down, quiet the mind, and focus on breathing have a naturally relaxing effect that also reduces stress and reduces the release of stress hormones in the body (Reivich & Shatte, 2002). Many people find great benefit in taking meditation, breathing exercises, or mind-body movement classes at the spa for the purposes of relaxation and stress-relief. A recent study of brain scans of yoga practitioners found lower levels of brain activity associated with depression and anxiety as compared to a walking control group (Streeter, et al., 2010).

Fitness and Exercise

While I have already covered the benefits of physical exercise in great detail, it is worthwhile to also highlight the role of physical activity in combating stress. When people are asked why they exercise, they often respond, "Because it makes me feel good" (Mutrie & Faulkner, 2004, p. 152). One of the ways that exercise makes people feel better is by alleviating the feelings of stress. People who are more active generally report feeling fewer symptoms of anxiety and less emotional distress. Regular exercise seems to have an impact on people's general stress levels ("trait anxiety"), and even a single bout of exercise will reduce anxious feelings immediately afterward ("state anxiety"; p. 153). There is also evidence that higher intensity exercise is quicker and more effective at reducing anxiety sensitivity (Ratey & Hagerman, 2008).

Exercise reduces the typical physiological reactivity to stressors (blood pressure, muscle tension, etc.) and also helps the body recover more quickly after being in a state of stress. Not all of the research has found these effects but at the very least it seems that exercise can serve as a *"buffer or coping strategy for psychosocial stress"* (Ratey & Hagerman, 2008, p. 154). One way that exercise helps to alleviate anxiety is by providing a healthy distraction from the sources of stress. Moving the body in a challenging way forces the mind to focus on something other than the underlying stressors.

Ironically, while helping people to relieve stress, exercise also puts stress on the body. By definition, exercise means we are challenging our muscles and the systems of the body, pushing them to do more than they are accustomed to. This is a good example of the "good stress" that I described earlier. The systems of the body are put under just enough stress that they are forced to develop themselves, becoming stronger than they were previously. In the muscular system, for example, exercise actually tears the muscles down slightly, creating minor injuries known as "adaptive micro-trauma" (Crowley & Lodge, 2004, p. 65). The body responds by activating its healing mechanisms and building the systems up to be stronger than ever so they can better withstand those stressors in the future.

The psychological impact of exercise is not much different. The medical community is accepting the fact that the mind can have an effect on the health of the body. The way we process the events in our lives mentally affects the body's physiological stress response with possible long term health consequences. Only more recently, scientists are beginning to believe that the actions of the body can also impact the health of the mind (Ratey & Hagerman, 2008). Exercising the body creates a stress response in the brain, influencing metabolic processes throughout the whole system, including those that facilitate "synaptic function" in the cells of the brain (p. 77). The hormones released during exercise not only help build muscles, they build new brain tissue as well, stimulating neurogenesis and neuroplasticity: growing new neurons and helping them bind together in new ways.

Pushing the body requires mental toughness as well. Committing to a regular exercise program requires self-control, perseverance and a strength of will to push through experiences that don't always feel good while they are occurring. But overcoming those mental challenges develops psychological resources that make people stronger and more resilient. They have greater feelings of control, self-efficacy, and self-mastery that help them to better handle stress from a variety of sources (Ratey & Hagerman, 2008).

Stress and Nutrition

Spas can also help their clients to handle stress through recommendations on healthful eating and food preparation. In January of 2004, the American Psychological Association's *Monitor* was dedicated to obesity and said that "high stress rates play a major role in the obesity epidemic" (as cited in Charlesworth & Nathan, 2004, p. 328). Responding to stress puts increasing demands on all the systems of the body, and it is essential that the right nutrients are available to support that. Spas that promote healthy eating can help their clients to strengthen their immune system, promote good health, avoid illness and disease, and deliver sufficient energy to help them perform at their best even when confronting challenges (p. 329).

The relationship between diet and stress is a two way street. Not only does a healthy diet provide the nourishment that is necessary to handle the stress response, but too much stress can also interfere with a healthy diet. High levels of stress lead people to turn to overeating, bad eating habits, and excessive consumption of alcohol as coping strategies (Charlesworth & Nathan, 2004, p. 330). When spas help people deal with stress in a healthy way, their health benefits not only come from avoiding the negative impacts of the stress response, but from being able to maintain a healthy lifestyle in a more confident and relaxed manner (more on this when we discuss lifestyle behaviors in Chapter 6.)

Happiness and Stress

Many of the links between health and happiness previously discussed are attributed to the ability of positive emotions to somehow protect us from the ravages of stress.

The "Stress Buffering Model" suggests that positive emotions protect us from stress by boosting the relaxation response, strengthening social relationships and motivating positive health behaviors.

In another proposed model, the "Enhanced Allostasis Model" (Bower, et al., 2009), "allostasis" refers to the body's ability to adapt to and recover from stress. This model identifies four ways that positive psychological processes might improve physiological responses to stress:

1.   "Fewer 'Hits'" i.e., less occurrences trigger a stress response.
2.   "Rapid Habituation" i.e., quicker adaptation to repetitive exposure to a stressor.
3.   "Rapid Recovery" i.e., bounce back more quickly from a stressful response.
4.   "Lower Tonic Arousal" i.e., stress system baseline is at a lower level in general.

Positive emotions contribute to health in a variety of ways: by opening our minds to possibilities, encouraging positive behaviors, facilitating supportive social networks and improving our physiological responses to stress. This is important information for the world of spas because it suggests that even if all we do is make people feel good, we are contributing positively to their health.

Pampering versus Wellness

I recently spoke at the New York Spa Alliance annual symposium (McCarthy, 2010). The theme of the symposium was "Pampering versus Wellness," a debate that has been raging in the spa industry for the past few years. Actually, it hasn't been much of a debate, since most people in the spa industry have turned their back on pampering and prefer to send the message that "spas are about wellness not pampering."

This is a dialogue that is based on fear. In a competitive marketplace where consumers are increasingly reluctant to spend their money on frivolity, it is critical for the world of spas to establish its importance to the welfare of its customers. The spa industry is challenged by the marketplace to show what it is made of and professionals rallied around the question, "Are we about pampering or about wellness?" Given those two choices, the industry did the only thing it could. It chose wellness. Pampering be damned.

The problem is that the whole pampering versus wellness debate is based on a false dichotomy. It presumes that you have to be about *either* pampering *or* wellness, but spas are about both. Not only is pampering an important part of the spa experience, it is an *essential* part of what makes up a spa. And as science solidifies these links between health and happiness and the stress-buffering nature of positive emotions, it seems safe to say that making people feel good is one way to help them be well.

Chapter 6
The Spa Lifestyle

Left to their own devices, most people "make pretty bad decisions" when it comes to the lifestyle choices that effect their health or happiness. The poor health behaviors that people incorporate into their lifestyle are "a leading cause of preventable morbidity and mortality" (Thaler & Sunstein, 2008, p. 5). As an example, Americans continue to get more and more overweight. Obesity rates for adults have doubled since 1980 with more than one third being classified as obese (defined as having greater than 30% body fat; Centers for Disease Control and Prevention, 2009). Obesity comes at a great economic cost with obesity associated medical costs rising to 9% of all U.S. medical costs (from 6.5% in 1998; Walker, 2009). The health and economic costs of obesity are felt most severely by the affected individuals, who spend 43% more for health care than normal weight patients.

It is hard to imagine that this growing phenomenon of obesity is simply due to ignorance of what is healthy. People need help and guidance in order to make good health decisions (Thaler & Sunstein, 2008). In spite of this, because of modern medicine's emphasis on pathology over prevention, interventions designed to address behavior are "underutilized in health care settings." In the U.S., changing health behaviors has been said to have the greatest potential of any other kind of medical approach "for improving the quality of life across diverse populations" (Whitlock, Orleans, Pender & Allan, 2002, p. 268).

One of the challenges in the medical system has been that doctors tend to be pessimistic about their own patients' ability to change (Prochaska, Norcross & Diclemente, 1994). This pessimism has serious health consequences to the general population since research shows that brief behavioral counseling interventions by physicians could make a substantial impact on health problems caused by risky behaviors such as smoking, poor diet, physical inactivity, inappropriate alcohol consumption, and unprotected sex (Whitlock, Orleans, Pender & Allan, 2002). Spas have an opportunity to provide a great service for their clients by educating them on healthy lifestyle behaviors in a way that they may not be getting from their physicians.

Spas in general have a greater focus on prevention and should be armed with a basic understanding of the science and research behind behavior change. This knowledge will help spa therapists to be more optimistic about the impact they can have when doling out advice to clients. Research on medical clinicians has shown that when they do give advice on health behaviors, it is associated with increased efforts towards behavior change and has been effective in changing behavior towards smoking, drinking and cardiovascular risk factors such as smoking and exercise. Patients who received this kind of advice also were more satisfied with the level of care they received (Whitlock, Orleans, Pender & Allan, 2002). People visit spas as a part of a healthy lifestyle. Understanding the psychological research on behavior change, spas can better assist their clients in making healthy lifestyle decisions and adopting healthy behaviors.

The Science of Changing Behavior

The Psychology of Behavior Change

Because of the potential beneficial outcomes of lifestyle changes, this has been a primary area of study and application in the field of psychology. The psychology of health behavior change can be divided into two major constructs: first, a "motivation phase," which is important for establishing the right health goals that a person should strive for; and second, a "volition phase," where actions are taken towards pursuit of those goals (Reuter, Ziegelmann, Wiedemann & Lippke, 2008, p. 194).

Perhaps what is most important is to recognize that self-change is possible and some people are clearly better at it than others. Most of the research comes from observing those who have successfully changed their behaviors to understand the processes and strategies that allowed them to do it. That being said, change does not occur quickly or easily. People often struggle to change their health behaviors and relapse is the norm and not the exception (Prochaska, Norcross & Diclemente, 1994). If spas really want to help their clients to live a healthy lifestyle, they need to be engaged for the long haul and should become familiar with a broad range of research from different theories of psychology that are useful for understanding behavior change.

The Stages of Change

When working with people on changing their behavior, it is necessary to identify and understand exactly where they are in the process. Experts in changing behavior have identified five stages that people go through when attempting to change their behavior. The first stage is "pre-contemplation," which means the person is not even ready to begin thinking about changing their lifestyle. They may prefer "ignorant bliss" over the harsh realities of seeing the problems they have that need fixing. An outside observer might describe this person as being "in denial" or as feeling demoralized and helpless about changing their behavior. People in a pre-contemplation stage tend to blame others (or external factors) for their problems and they do not appreciate the people close to them who are "pestering them" to change (Prochaska, Norcross & DiClemente, 2006).

Spas who are working with people in the pre-contemplation stage won't be successful at changing behaviors that their clients are not ready to change. The spa's goal should be to help people get to a space where they can just begin contemplating the need to change. "Consciousness-raising" is the most important process during this stage, so mindfulness practices and other techniques to raise one's level of self-awareness can be beneficial. Also spas can be helpful by educating their clients on the health risks of their behaviors and providing them information that might help them to shift their thinking.

The second stage of behavior change is "contemplation," in which people begin to acknowledge the problem and wrestle with whether or not this is something they should actively change. People can spend years or even decades in this stage, like smokers that know smoking is bad for them but never seriously takes steps to quit. Consciousness-raising can continue to be a beneficial strategy for contemplators, but spas should also consider how to tap into the person's emotions to raise the awareness of the problem to a serious enough level to warrant action. Sometimes this doesn't occur until someone close to them has serious health consequences from similar behaviors. But spas can encourage people to continually practice "self-reevaluation" to encourage them to identify where their behavior might conflict with their core values (Prochaska, Norcross & DiClemente, 2006).

When people move through the contemplation stage they move into "preparation." In preparation, they have decided to commit to changing and have plans to change their lifestyle in the near future. They may still be struggling with the decision or with converting the decision into action (Prochaska, Norcross & DiClemente, 2006). Spa clients in this stage need to take responsibility for the change. Spas can strive to teach their clients that only they can change themselves. The locus of control has to shift internally so people will commit to the actions required for lasting change. Spas should also encourage their clients in the preparation stage to make their plans public, in order to increase the level of commitment to taking action.

The "action" stage means the client is committing both time and energy to actually change their behavior. This is the most visible stage as clear changes begin to take place in the person's lifestyle. This can also be a challenging stage, and many people find they slide back to an earlier stage before creating a lasting change in their health behaviors (Prochaska, Norcross & DiClemente, 2006).

Spas can help people in the action stage by suggesting different strategies that they can implement to be successful. "Countering" for example, is a strategy of substituting a healthy response for an unhealthy one (like going to the gym when feeling upset, rather than the refrigerator). Restructuring the environment (like keeping unhealthy snacks out of the house, or staying out of bars if someone is trying to drink less) to facilitate the new behavior is another viable behavior change strategy. Spas can not only suggest that their clients reward themselves for their successes in this stage, but can also be instrumental in providing those rewards. Spa programs can have built in rewards (like a massage or other enjoyable treatment) that people get when certain health goals are reached (Prochaska, Norcross & DiClemente, 2006).

When the action becomes sustained, then the person's lifestyle has truly changed. The person now moves into the "maintenance" stage. In the maintenance stage, people work to consolidate the gains made in the previous stages and incorporate them fully into their lifestyle. This is a long process and still requires a strong commitment to avoid any relapse or backsliding to the familiar unhealthy behaviors of the past. Spas can continue to suggest the strategies above and also help their clients by being a part of their support network of helping relationships to keep them on track. Facilitating social networks among spa clients is another way that spas can help people in the maintenance stage (Prochaska, Norcross & DiClemente, 2006).

Changing behavior is not easy, and people rarely move through these stages without having relapses back to earlier stages (Prochaska, Norcross & DiClemente, 2006). Understanding that relapse is the rule rather than the exception can help people to pick themselves up and get back into the change process rather than becoming frustrated by a feeling of failure, guilt or shame (p. 48). Spas can better serve people by recognizing what stage they are at in the process and providing the right strategy for that moment. People's needs differ as they go through the stages and so it is ideal if spas can personalize the support provided to the specific needs of their clients.

Self-Determination Theory

Self-determination theory (SDT; Brown and Ryan, 2004) suggests that the motivations that drive behavior "have important consequences for healthy behavioral regulation and psychological wellbeing" (p. 105). Behavior that is driven by autonomous motivation (coming from within the individual) is said to be "self-determined" and may lead to more positive outcomes. Some people will visit spas volitionally and with a strong intrinsic motivation to improve their health and wellbeing. Others might be there for more extrinsic reasons, accompanying a friend or redeeming a gift from someone else. Spas should evaluate the motivation of their clients before making lifestyle recommendations or interventions.

Developing self-awareness may be the first step in making positive change in someone's life. The "lack of attention to one's behavior" can lead to a state of autopilot that may make it difficult to accomplish great things, but consciousness, "can introduce an element of self-direction" into a person's actions (pp. 115-116). Spas often offer various assessments to help people identify areas in need of improvement and also help their clients spend time in quiet reflection so they can evaluate their own wellbeing.

One thing that spas do well is to create wellness interventions that are incredibly pleasurable and enjoyable. Unlike other healing institutions in modern society, spas are places that people look forward to visiting and enjoy their time while they are there. For many people, most healthful behaviors (dieting, rigorous exercise, medical treatments) are thought to be unenjoyable, but are things that we "should" do (either because of societal pressure or because of the health risks of failing to do them). Spas, by making their experiences extremely enjoyable, are able to help people generate their own intrinsic motivation for maintaining healthy lifestyle behaviors.

Intrinsic motivation is associated with numerous positive outcomes and occurs when we are "doing an activity for its inherent enjoyment and interest" (Brown & Ryan, 2004, p. 107). Sometimes those who are dragged to the spa by their friends, find that it is more enjoyable than they realized and become loyal customers. Many male spa-goers, for example, experience their first treatment while with a partner, but once indoctrinated, they become even more of a regular spa-goer (ISPA, 2006b). It is possible, through "internalization and integration," to make extrinsically motivated behaviors more autonomous (Brown & Ryan, 2004, p. 111).

Spas also encourage social interaction in a way that supports behavior change. Most spas today offer couples' experiences as well as being an outlet for small groups of friends (usually women) to come together and share in an enjoyable, healthy experience. The social aspect of spas is important to how a spa lifestyle is learned since "feelings of relatedness or connectedness" within a social support structure can aid in changing behavior (Brown & Ryan, 2004, p. 111).

Motivational Interviewing

Dr. Timothy Anstiss has been teaching "Motivational Interviewing" as a way for spa and fitness professionals to drive behavior change in their clients by facilitating greater intrinsic motivation towards the desired improvements. Motivational Interviewing (MI) is an evidence-based approach to patient centered care. The skills required include "asking skillful open ended questions; making well-timed affirmations; making frequent and skillful reflective listening statements; and using summaries to communicate understanding" (Anstiss, 2009).

The principles of MI can be remembered by using the acronym RULE:

- **Resist** the righting reflex — resist the natural urge to try and fix a client's behavior. They have to come to the solution themselves.
- **Understand** your patient's dilemma and motivations — use empathy and compassion to see things from the client's perspective
- **Listen** to your patients or clients — you are not telling them how to change but listening to their perspective and helping them to see any discrepancies between their current behaviors and values.
- **Empower** your patients — by boosting the confidence of your clients you are helping them develop the self-efficacy needed to create change for themselves.

Motivational Interviewing allows practitioners to incorporate client preferences into their treatment. And since MI is not about doling out prescriptions or advice, there is no certification required to help encourage someone to find the change they need to create for themselves. By boosting feelings of autonomy and competence, it creates a more self-determined approach to behavior change. Intrinsically motivated change is easier to bring about and more likely to "stick."

Mindfulness and Self-Compassion

Spas also teach and encourage "mindfulness," which is another way to help people develop more consciousness about their motivations and behaviors. Mindfulness has been defined as "the clean and single-minded awareness of what actually happens to us and in us at the successive moments of perception" (Nayanaponika Thera, 1972 as cited in Brown & Ryan, 2002). Mindfulness is a skill that can be cultivated and is often practiced through meditation or through being more meditative or "present" during day to day tasks (Kabat-Zinn, 1994; Weiss, 2004). By being more mindful or aware of their own reactions to stimuli, people can consciously shift towards more self-determined, autonomous behavior.

Mindfulness serves as a monitoring function so people can learn more about their own behavior and adapt accordingly. Jon Kabat-Zinn, one of the world's leading experts on mindfulness describes it in this way:

> It has everything to do with waking up and living in harmony with oneself and with the world. It has to do with examining who we are, with questioning our view of the world and our place in it, and with cultivating some appreciation for the fullness of each moment we are alive (1994, p. 3).

Researchers who have studied mindfulness have found it to be related to greater autonomous regulation of behavior. This is at least in part due to giving people an opportunity to reflect and choose their behaviors rather than simply acting on auto-pilot. One way that mindfulness predicts higher wellbeing is by facilitating people's ability to self-regulate their own behavior (Brown & Ryan, 2002).

Recently, researchers have been narrowing in on "self-compassion" as a key component of mindfulness that may be strongly tied to the positive outcomes of a mindfulness practice. Kristin Neff from University of Texas has driven much of the research on self-compassion, which she defines as "an alternative conceptualization of a healthy attitude toward oneself" (Neff, 2003, p. 85). She identified self-kindness as one of the primary components of self-compassion, and it's hard to imagine a better act of self-kindness than indulging in a relaxing and pleasurable spa experience. A recent study found that self-compassion "is a robust predictor of symptom severity and quality of life, accounting for as much as ten times more unique variance in the dependent variables than mindfulness" (Van Dam, et al., 2010, p. 123).

Developing Willpower

Self-regulation

Increasing self-awareness and having social support structures to model autonomous behaviors are two ways that individuals learn self-regulation (Brown & Ryan, 2004). Self-regulation (also known as "self-control" or "willpower") is how a person "exerts control over his or her own responses so as to pursue goals and live up to standards" (Peterson & Seligman, 2004, p. 500). Many of the skills that spas attempt to teach (healthy eating, exercise, bathing and skincare rituals, meditation, etc.) require self-regulation on the part of the participant if they are to be maintained on any kind of ongoing basis. To eat healthfully for example, a person must practice self-regulation to "restrain themselves from carrying out impulses and desires" that may lead them towards unhealthy (but delicious) foods (p. 500).

The challenge of self-regulation is evident to anyone who has ever made New Year's resolutions and found that they were all broken before February. For as far back as the ancient Greeks, this weakness or lack of ability to see a goal through to its completion has been described as a "deficiency of will" (Mischel, Cantor & Feldman, 1996). And so the concept of having control over one's will or "willpower" has evolved to describe how someone resists "the temptation of immediate gratification for the sake of long term goals" (p. 330).

Psychology has strived to understand the individual differences between people that have greater self-regulatory control than others. Walter Mischel, an American psychologist who has studied willpower extensively, noted that this skill or strength varies greatly from one person to the next:

> Although some individuals seem able to adhere to stringent diets,
> to give up cigarettes after years of smoking them addictively, or to
> continue to labor for distant goals even when sorely frustrated,
> others fail at these efforts although failure may cost them their
> health and lives (1996, p. 197).

Mischel sought to understand how it was that some people are better than
others at turning their "good intentions" into reality, even in the face of
great challenge.

Self-regulation occurs when people override their initial responses to
a stimulus to "direct their thought processes in directions other than where
their minds naturally wander" (Peterson & Seligman, 2004, p. 500). Self-
regulation helps people to be more successful in attaining their goals
because they are able to avoid distractions that may keep them from
initiating and then sticking with goal directed behaviors. People who have
this strength are better able to control their environment and their
emotions so that their behavior stays on track towards desired outcomes
(Gollwitzer, 1999).

A lack of self-regulation may be one of the biggest factors in "nearly
all the personal and social problems that currently plague citizens of the
modern, developed world" including drug addiction, alcoholism,
smoking, failure to exercise regularly and overeating (Peterson &
Seligman, 2004, p. 506). A high level of self-control, on the other hand, is
related with doing better in school, being more psychologically well
adjusted, and having better relationships with others. People who have
this strength are less likely to abuse alcohol or drugs, and are less likely to
have eating disorders (Peterson & Seligman, 2004).

Some of the initial research on this area of study centered on "delay of
gratification" (Mischel & Ebbesen, 1970 as cited in Peterson & Seligman,
2004, p. 500). These studies measured a child's ability to resist a tempting
immediate reward (like a marshmallow or a cookie) in exchange for
receiving a greater reward a little later. In essence, this is the same
decision spa consumers are forced to make when they have to choose
between going to the gym or going out with friends; between ordering a
salad or french fries with their lunch; between waking up and meditating
for twenty minutes before going to work versus hitting the snooze button
on the alarm clock. The ability to delay gratification is so profoundly
important that differences in pre-schoolers' ability to delay eating treats
(measured in seconds before caving in to the temptation of the cookie or
marshmallow) predicted differences in academic achievement and
parental ratings over ten years later (Mischel, 1996). If spas could help

teach their clients how to develop their strength of self-regulation and their ability to delay gratification, they would be arming them with a valuable tool for creating a healthy lifestyle.

Psychologists have identified two processes that take place when a person tries to suppress an unwanted thought (Wegner & Pennebaker, 1993 as cited in Peterson & Seligman, 2004). A monitoring process scans the environment looking for temptations, and when a temptation is identified, an operating process overrides the urge to indulge in it. One problem with the way the mind handles these processes is that it becomes more and more adept at scanning the environment in search of temptations. As soon as the individual lets their guard down, their mind is drawn to these thoughts more than ever and so they have a "rebound effect" (p. 502). This is one reason why dieters find that even once they lose the weight it may be difficult to keep it off.

Research on delay of gratification found that, contrary to the original hypothesis that focusing on the source of temptation would increase the motivation to wait for a better reward, child participants were better able to exert control when they did not have the tempting reward in sight (Mischel, 1996). The children who were most successful at resisting the urges employed simple "purposeful self-distraction" strategies to divert themselves from thinking about the reward. They either focused on their intention to wait, reminding themselves of what they needed to do to earn the greater reward and what the negative consequences would be of not waiting. Or they simply engrossed themselves in other distracting activities to keep themselves from thinking about the tempting treat they were being lured with (p. 203).

Recently, some researchers have proposed a more mindful approach to resisting temptation. Rather than having subjects distract themselves from temptation, they encourage them to prepare for and remain aware of the urges that build within them. This concept is based on the idea that urges come in waves, so if people are aware that the urge will soon pass, they can simply "ride the wave" and wait for it to dissipate. Research on smokers has found that this mindfulness approach helped people cave in less often, although they experienced the same amount of temptation as those in a control group (Bowen & Marlatt, 2009).

Some psychologists (Baumeister, Gailliot, Dewall & Oaten, 2006) have suggested that practice is the key to developing self-control. Self-regulation "resembles a muscle" (p. 1776) and it can be strengthened by exercising those skills. Numerous studies show how these mechanisms can be fatigued after depletion from performing self-regulating tasks, but that "in the long run, exercise strengthens them" (p. 1779). Spas could

develop interventions around facilitating the practice of these skills. For
example some research has shown that putting people onto an exercise
program over time improved their self-regulatory abilities (Oaten &
Cheng, 2006).

Practicing self-regulation extends into other domains so participants
who practiced adherence to an exercise program also seemed to get better
at avoiding smoking, cutting back on alcohol and caffeine consumption
and even seemingly unrelated areas such as studying more or washing
dishes more regularly. Spas can help their clients to practice self-
regulation, which "given the broad range of positive outcomes associated
with self-regulation, they might well find that enhancing self-regulatory
strength would be a useful and valuable way to promote health,
happiness, and other positive outcomes" (Baumeister, Gailliot, Dewall &
Oaten, 2006, p. 1780).

Because self-regulation is like a muscle, it means that giving spa
guests opportunities to practice self-regulatory behaviors will help them to
strengthen these skills and integrate them into their day to day lives. This
strategy can backfire however, because like a muscle, the self-regulatory
systems can also become fatigued (Baumeister et al., 2006). A client who
comes home from a week of regulating themselves at the spa may find that
their self-control has been spent and that they are unable to resist the urge
to binge on sweet or fatty foods as soon as they return home. Spas can
help their guests avoid these rebounds by educating them on the nature of
their self-regulation mechanisms so they know to continue exercising these
skills, but to be careful to avoid temptations when their regulatory
"muscles" may be fatigued.

Spas can also assist their clients in practicing self-control by
suggesting "monitoring" strategies so that they continue to be aware of
their goals and the behaviors they want to stick to. This can be done via
journal writing or by engaging other people to help keep them on track
and remind them when they seem to deviate from their goals. Because
self-regulation often involves sacrificing immediate gratification in
exchange for some long-term health benefit, spas can also teach their
clients how to be more future-minded, and to focus on the greater
outcomes that are gained in the long run by exercising control.

The idea of developing willpower might seem like training someone
to be able to withstand great discomfort. But the reality is that people who
have a high strength of self-control do not necessarily just grin and bear
miserable situations all the time. Children in the delay of gratification
studies, for example, "invented ways to help themselves achieve their goal
without becoming too upset and discouraged" (Mischel, 1996, p. 209).

They were able to delay gratification by distracting themselves with other enjoyable activities.

This is a somewhat different view of the concept of "willpower," which can be misleading if it is assumed that making healthful decisions is always going to be the less pleasant option. I do not think people who have a high strength of self-control necessarily exert a massive effort over their will in an almighty effort to stay on their intended course. Some people, for example, who are said to have a lot of willpower, may simply have a smaller delta between what they *should* do and what they *want* to do. People who don't like sweets, for example, do not need willpower to avoid sugary foods. And people who love to exercise do not need to do any mental gymnastics to convince themselves to go to the gym. One way to think about increasing willpower in spa guests is to think about their mindset. How can people's beliefs and thought patterns help them *want* to do the things they *should* do?

Mindset

The way people view their own ability to change, learn, or grow has a substantial impact on their ability to self-regulate. Research shows that people have different beliefs about their own abilities to change, and furthermore, that these beliefs can affect people's abilities to change and grow. The question at the root of these powerful beliefs is whether or not our behavior and lifestyle are more determined by our genetics or by our interactions with our environment. While this is a debate that has been played out in scientific research for decades, there is no conclusive answer to the *nature versus nurture* controversy. What seems to be clear is that who we become is a function of both: the genetic recipe of strengths and weaknesses that we inherit from others, and our ability to learn and grow by interacting with our environment (Dweck, 2006).

Our *beliefs* about the importance of genetics versus individual effort have a tremendous impact on the accomplishments and success we are able to achieve. Carol Dweck, a leading researcher in this area, refers to these varying belief systems as our "mindset" (2006). When people believe that they are stuck with the hand they are dealt and that there is little they can do to change (i.e., their "qualities are carved in stone"), this is referred to as a "fixed mindset" (p. 6). A "growth mindset" on the other hand, is the belief that a person's basic qualities can be cultivated through individual effort (p. 7). Those with a fixed mindset believe that people have "natural talent" i.e., "you either have it or you don't." Those with a growth mindset believe that we are malleable beings and that we can improve through practice, experience and learning.

These different approaches to growth and learning affect the ways that people process and respond to information. Those who have a fixed mindset, because they don't believe they can actually change their abilities, are more interested in maintaining appearances that show their good qualities. They are concerned with how they will be judged by others. Those with a growth mindset, on the other hand, would be willing to put themselves into a challenging situation, even though it may make them appear foolish, if it gives them the opportunity to learn or grow. They are concerned with self-improvement (Dweck, 2006).

These sets of beliefs are related to self-control because those with a fixed mindset believe you are either "strong and you have willpower" or you are "weak and don't have willpower" (Dweck, 2006, p. 239). This runs contrary to the research indicating that self-regulation is malleable and can be strengthened "like a muscle" (Baumeister, Gailliot, Dewall & Oaten, 2006). When a person is trying to change their lifestyle, a fixed mindset will lead them to avoid challenging themselves, underestimate the importance of effort, ignore useful negative feedback and feel threatened by the success of others. They will be much more likely to quit or to "plateau early and achieve less than their full potential" (Holmes, 2007; Dweck, 2006). Someone who has a growth mindset is more likely to value the effort required to bring about a true change in lifestyle that can ultimately have a positive effect on health.

The good news is that research indicates it is possible for a person to change their mindset. For spas that are interested in changing their clients' behaviors, this is useful strategy to be aware of. If spas can help their clients to develop a growth mindset they can help them to embrace the challenge they are confronting, to persist in the face of setbacks, to learn from others, and to not shy away from the effort required to bring about change (Holmes, 2007; Dweck, 2006).

To help clients develop more of a growth mindset, spas should pay attention to the "messages about success and failure" that they communicate to their clients (Dweck, 2006, p. 174). Centering praise on process and growth (rather than on talent or ability) encourages people to adopt a growth mindset. When spas recognize the effort that their clients are putting in, it encourages them to continue taking the steps that lead to a healthy change in lifestyle. Messages about failure are equally important. Spas should encourage their clients to learn from their mistakes and setbacks and evaluate what steps they can take or how they could direct their efforts to get back on track.

According to Dweck, "just learning about the growth mindset can cause a big shift in the way people think about themselves" (2006, p. 216). So educating clients about the different types of belief systems and how they can affect our lifestyle choices could make a difference. Sharing success stories of other clients who have been able to change helps provide evidence to support the validity of a growth mindset. Spas can help their clients by telling stories of those who have succeeded at making substantial change in their lives or even by introducing them to people who can model the level of effort and commitment necessary to make lasting change.

Self-efficacy

Another concept from the field of psychology that is related to mindset and pertinent for improving human health and happiness is self-efficacy theory, which suggests that believing in one's own capabilities increases the likelihood of positive outcomes from one's actions (Maddux, 2002). People who believe in their "capabilities to produce desired effects by their own actions" are more likely to engage in actions that will bring them greater benefit and are more likely to persevere in spite of difficulties (Bandura, 1997 as cited in Maddux, 2002, p. 277). Self-efficacy beliefs are not a perception of skill or an expected outcome, but rather the belief that we have the capability to accomplish an objective within a specific set of circumstances. When people doubt their own abilities to change, it can "place a ceiling" on how much positive growth they will be able to accomplish (Reivich & Shatte, 2002, p. 145).

Similar to the research on mindset, self-efficacy researchers also find that people typically overestimate the role of talent in accomplishment "while underestimating the role of self-regulation" (p. 285). The more self-efficacy beliefs one has, "the loftier will be the goals" that they will attempt to take on (p. 282). Once those goals are set, a high belief in one's capabilities will lead to increased "persistence in the face of challenge and obstacles." We know empirically that perseverance is associated with achieving difficult goals (Duckworth, Peterson, Matthews & Kelly, 2007). Positive interventions designed to encourage self-efficacy can create a virtuous cycle where self-beliefs are elevated, leading to more positive outcomes, leading to higher self-beliefs, and so on. These kinds of strategies are based on "enablement," defined as "providing people with skills for selecting and attaining the life they desire" (Maddux, 2004, p. 285).

Self-efficacy has been shown to be a substantial determinant of physical health. People with high self-efficacy are more likely to adopt healthy behaviors and stop unhealthy behaviors. They are also more likely to maintain healthy behaviors even when confronted with difficulties. Researchers have found that enhancing self-efficacy "is crucial to successful change and maintenance of virtually every behavior crucial to health, including exercise, diet, stress management . . ." (Maddux, 2004, p. 281).

Self-efficacy training has been shown to improve mood, lower anxiety, reduce pain and improve metabolic health measurements (Kleinman, Guess, & Wilentz, 2002). Self-efficacy is also an essential ingredient for "streering through" chronic stress (Reivich & Shatte, 2002). By making people feel more in control of their situations, self-efficacy beliefs also improve the body's ability to handle stress, which has a direct impact on the human immune system (Maddux, 2004).

Self-efficacy beliefs can be developed in a number of ways. People can cultivate self-efficacy via "verbal persuasion" through coaching and guidance (i.e., "you can do it!"). People can also use visualization techniques to imagine success and grow their feelings of self-efficacy in that way. But the most potent way to develop these beliefs is based on one's own historic attempts at setting goals and then achieving them successfully. When someone successfully controls their own outcomes and environments they begin to feel more capable of repeating those successes in the future (Maddux, 2004).

Goal Theory

Goal Setting and Behavior Change

Spas can help people change their behavior by helping them to set goals and focus on their intentions. The Aristotelian concept of "final causality," which is at the root of goal setting theory, is based on the idea that intention is related to outcome (Melchert, 2002). The reason why we attempt to regulate our thoughts, emotions and actions is because we want to achieve specific desired outcomes (Maddux, 2004).

Goal setting theorists have studied the effect of intentionality and free-will on the outcomes of human behavior and have found a number of measurable ways in which goals influence human achievement. The goals we set, and the processes we follow to achieve those goals, make a difference in the accomplishments we achieve. Goals that are too vague ("do your best" goals), for example, do not typically yield good results, even when the challenge level is high. Goals that are difficult to attain *and* specific, on the other hand, lead to the highest levels of performance. These kinds of goals elicit higher levels of commitment, pushing us to strive through in spite of challenges we may confront along the way (Locke, 1996). Increasing commitment can be achieved through interventions designed to adjust the goal to be more attainable, to improve capacity to reach the goal, or to give expressions of confidence to boost the perspective of the person's ability to achieve the goal (Locke, 1996).

Specific goals are more effective because it is easier for someone to monitor their own progress towards the goal and adjust their behaviors based on specific measures of goal attainment. For this same reason, goal attainment is also more likely when goals are proximal or short-term, rather than distal or long-term (Bandura & Schunk, 1981, as cited in Gollwitzer, 1999). And as indicated by the research on "mindset" mentioned above, "learning goals" (intending to grow and improve) tend to yield better results than "performance goals" (intending to determine or demonstrate capabilities; Gollwitzer, 1999, p. 493; Dweck, 2006). Consistent with the spa industry's emphasis on promoting wellness rather than disease prevention, promotion goals (focused on "the presence or absence of positive outcomes") are more effective than prevention goals (focused on "the presence or absence of negative outcomes"; Higgins, 1997 as cited in Gollwitzer, 1999, p. 494).

Not only can effective goal setting help spa clients reach their health goals, but psychological research supports the idea that "goal attainment leads to positive wellbeing" (Sagiv, Roccas & Hazan, 2004, p. 75). Helping clients to set and attain goals in any area of their lives (beyond health) can have a positive impact on overall wellness.

Wanting What You Want to Want

One goal setting exercise from the field of positive psychology is called, "Wanting What You Want to Want" (J. O. Pawelski, MAPP 602 lecture, October 5, 2008). In this exercise individuals choose what they want to want more or want less, and partners coach them to help them focus on the things that would help them to change their level of want in the desired direction. I have found that this activity is helpful not only in increasing motivation towards goals that people want but also in gaining clarity around what goals are most meaningful to them.

This intervention could also be applied in a spa setting. Many spas, especially destination spas, where people spend a significant amount of time working on certain health and wellness goals, might ask people to establish some goals for their spa visit. But asking "what do you want to want more?" would help to emphasize the importance of the individual's motivation in achieving those goals. There is a distinction between saying, "I'm going to a spa because I want to lose weight by exercising" versus "I'm going to a spa because I *want to want* to exercise more in order to lose weight." In the latter version, the implication is that the spa's role is not to help the client lose weight, but to help increase their motivation so they can practice the behaviors they need to in order to lose weight and maintain their health on an ongoing basis.

Once the spa knows what their client wants to want more, they can work with them to improve their desire. The spa therapist can help the client to focus on increasing these desires by asking open-ended questions such as, "What would you need to think about in order to want this more?" One of the good things about this intervention is it clearly leaves the participant responsible for their own outcomes.

This is important because experts on goal setting believe that striving for "self-concordant" goals not only led to a greater sense of wellbeing, but a greater chance of attaining the goals. Self-concordant goals are defined as "goals derived from intrinsic or identified motives, rather than introjected or extrinsic motives (Sheldon and Elliot, 1999 as cited in Sagiv, Roccas & Hazan, 2004, p. 73). Having intrinsic motivation and self-concordant goals can improve the outcome by improving a sense of self-efficacy, self control and perseverance.

Writing Goals Down

Some spas teach journal writing classes, which is a good opportunity to help clients express and formalize goals. One technique that spas can use to increase hope and goal setting is the "best possible self" (BPS) exercise. In this intervention, participants are asked to write about a future vision of themselves at their best. Writing has been known for years to have a therapeutic effect on health, although this was once attributed to the releasing of pent up negative emotions. The BPS exercise encourages people to write about a positive experience. This kind of writing has been shown to have the same or better health benefits of other types of (more negative) journaling, while also increasing happiness, optimism, and subjective wellbeing (King, 2001).

Hope Theory

By helping spa-goers identify their goals and creating pathways towards achieving them, spas can give people a sense of hope that will motivate them to continue engaging in healthful activities into the future. Increasingly, hope is being viewed as a serious health intervention by the medical community. Psychiatrist Harold Bursztajn tells the story of doctors in the Lodz ghettoes of Poland during World War II, healing people without medicine or equipment. "These doctors gave people hope," he said. "The doctor becomes the medicine." Modern doctors are learning from these stories of healers successfully using only kindness and compassion to treat their patients (Forman, 2009).

The benefits of hope are many, including higher health, better school and athletic performance, better problem-solving skills and better psychological adjustment (Snyder, 2002; Snyder, Cheavens, & Michael, 1999 [as cited in Snyder, et al., 2006, p. 394]). Spa therapies should be designed with a focus on "training people to increase hope," in the tradition of all good therapy frameworks. Spa-goers will experience enhanced wellbeing when they "have well-developed goals and believe that they have the capacities and resources to reach those goals" (Snyder et al., 2006, p. 185). A sense of hope, once instilled, will help people to persevere with their health goals even when the going gets rough.

Perseverance and "Grit"

Research on "grit" suggests that one of the ways that goals lead to success is simply from good old-fashioned hard work and effort. Grit is defined as the "perseverance and passion for long-term goals" (Duckworth, Peterson, Matthews & Kelly, 2007, p. 1087). There is evidence that success at achieving goals comes from "sustained commitment," i.e., sticking to them over a long period of time. It may be that people who are successful at reaching their goals are not lucky, or smart, or talented, but rather have the tenacity or "grittiness" to persevere in pursuit of their goals long after others have given up (p. 1088).

For spas working with clients that are striving to attain specific health goals, the research on perseverance can inspire people to stay the course even when challenge and distraction may be pulling them in a different direction. People have to understand that changing behavior is not something that can be done quickly, and so a long-term approach can be beneficial. Gritty individuals are those who set challenging goals for themselves with extremely long-term objectives "and do not swerve from them—even in the absence of positive feedback" (Duckworth, Peterson, Matthews & Kelly, 2007, p. 1089).

A variety of studies have shown that this level of perseverance and commitment is associated with success in several outcomes. Grittiness is associated with better academic performance in students and a higher overall level of academic achievement in adults. Grit predicted retention in a rigorous military training program at West Point, and also predicted greater achievement in the Scripps National Spelling Bee. The evidence shows that success is determined by those who work harder and longer (Duckworth, Peterson, Matthews & Kelly, 2007). This is consistent with an earlier qualitative study on prodigies and experts that showed they spent at least ten years working several hours a day in order to become the best at what they do (Bloom, 1985 as cited in Duckworth, et al, 2007; Gladwell, 2009).

Spas should share this kind of information with their clients as a way of encouraging a growth mindset. Spa customers may want to change their body composition, improve their health, or eliminate unhealthy habits from their lifestyle. None of these changes are easy. The research shows that passion, commitment and time are all required to turn goals into reality. Spas help their clients achieve their health goals when they can instill a sense of passion, enlist a sense of commitment, and help them sustain effort over a long period of time.

Implementation Intentions

We have been reviewing all of the benefits that spa clients can achieve by focusing on and clarifying their wellness goals. This is very consistent with the philosophy of the spa world, which often turns not to scientific research, but to the *self-help* genre to support the basis for their offerings. I mentioned previously that many of the most popular self-help books written have promoted the idea that success in all domains of life comes from having positive intentions and keeping those intentions in focus (e.g., *The Secret* by Rhonda Byrne [2006], *The Power of Intention* by Wayne Dyer [2004], and *Spontaneous Fulfillment of Desire* by Deepak Chopra [2003]). These concepts are not without scientific basis, since psychologists for years have investigated the power of intention and have often found it to be a powerful predictor of behavior. The best way to predict if someone plans on going to the gym after work is simply to ask them what they intend to do. But when it comes to long term health goals, it seems that good intentions are only a part of the equation (Reuter, Ziegelmann, Wiedemann & Lippke, 2008).

Psychologists have identified an "intention-behavior gap," which shows that people "do not fully act upon their intentions." Human nature, as imperfect as it is, allows for people to forget their goals, be distracted by other ideas (for example more tempting but less healthy options), or fall into the rut of a habit that is counterproductive for attainment of the goal. To truly help people achieve their health goals, spas need to not only help people to set the right intentions in the motivation phase, but to also concentrate on the volition phase by giving people strategies for the "successful translation of intentions into action" (Reuter, Ziegelmann, Wiedemann & Lippke, 2008, p. 195).

Two different motivations at play in goal setting have been defined as "choice motivation" and "control motivation" (Kuhl, 1984 as cited in Mischel, Cantor & Feldman, 1996). Willpower is used both in "choice motivation" when choosing between two options (eat the cookie now, or go to the gym and have better health later), and in "control motivation" when exerting the effort to overcome any challenges to attain the goal that was chosen. Different individuals may have different types of self-regulation. Some may be better at choosing the right goals. Others may be better at following through on their chosen goal (Mischel, Cantor & Feldman, 1996).

For people to be successful at goal attainment, they must focus not only on their intended goals, but also on their "implementation intentions." Unlike goals, which identify the desired outcomes (i.e., clarifying "what you want"), implementation intentions clarify the "when, where and how" you will go about accomplishing it (Gollwitzer, 1999, p. 498). Implementation intentions facilitate greater self-control because they allow the person to decide in advance how they will handle specific situations. These "anticipative decisions" are easier to make because they can be thought through at a time when other stimuli that might distract from the intended outcome are not present. "Predeciding" how a goal should be implemented reduces the need for lengthy or stressful deliberations once a situation presents itself and thus the healthy behavior becomes more automatic (Gollwitzer, 1999, p. 494).

A spa can help a customer with their exercise goals, for example, by asking them when, where and how they plan to exercise. Many people set goals to exercise but never actually start on a program because they have never specified the details of how they will implement their intentions. Once the implementation intentions are established, the client needs only to wait for the situational cue (e.g., Monday at 5:30 p.m.), and they can more easily take action towards their goal. Studies have shown that setting implementation intentions is effective at helping people initiate actions towards their goals and ultimately attaining the desired outcomes (Gollwitzer, 1999).

The challenge with health promotion and disease-prevention goals is that the individual typically has to take on a negatively perceived activity immediately, in exchange for long-term benefits that won't be experienced for some time (Gollwitzer & Oettingen as cited in Gollwitzer, 1999). But research has shown that implementation intentions can help even in these kinds of long-term health goals. Health promotion studies on people who were asked to perform regular breast self-examinations (Orbell, Hodgkins, & Sheeran, 1997) or take a daily vitamin supplements (Sheeran & Orbell, 1999 as cited in Gollwitzer, 1999) showed greater results when the goals were established with specific implementation guidelines.

Another study on college students' participation in a vigorous exercise program found that implementation intentions improved participants' compliance far more than other motivation interventions focused on increasing self-efficacy or increasing perceived fear of heart disease from lack of exercise (Milne, Orbell, & Sheeran, 1999 as cited in Gollwitzer, 1999). Appeals to fear in other health promotion experiments (e.g., a smoking cessation program) have shown this tactic is much more effective at motivating participants when combined with specific goal implementation instructions (Leventhal, Singer, & Jones, 1965 as cited in Gollwitzer, 1999).

The motivation phase of goal setting is still a crucial first step. The implementation intentions add a "planning" phase that fills the gap in between intentions and behavior. Research on health behavior change showed that goal-setting and motivation increase planning activity. Furthermore, increased planning activities lead to greater changes in health behavior. The research shows a "causal chain" linking intention to planning to behavior (Reuter, Ziegelmann, Wiedemann & Lippke, 2008, p. 203).

Habits are beneficial as a way of automating healthy behaviors (or avoiding those habits that automate unhealthy behaviors). Implementation intentions are another way to automate healthy behaviors without the need to invest substantial amounts of time in practicing a new behavior. A person is able to "replace or mimic the effects of habit by forming implementation intentions" that mentally link the desired behavior to specific situational cues in the environment (Gollwitzer, 1999, p. 499).

Spas can help their clients create "instant habits" by helping them pre-decide how they will implement their goals when confronted with certain situations (i.e., being presented with a dessert menu or an unhealthy snack, feeling stressed or emotional, or being invited to the bar when on the way to the gym after work). These decision processes can help people to overcome existing negative habits that may have led them to behave differently when confronted with these cues. These mental procedures can be established very quickly, and once in place, they can last for a surprisingly long time (Gollwitzer, 1999, p. 499-500).

Habits

There is a huge amount of research in the psychology literature about how habits are formed. And because habits are the behaviors that people tend to turn to automatically, they can be a determining factor in the kind of lifestyle one leads. Health behavior truly becomes assimilated into a person's lifestyle when it becomes a habit. Habit formation is one reason why self-regulatory skills develop with sufficient practice: "People ought simply to get better at anything they do over and over as a result of habit formation, increased knowledge and understanding, increased liking from familiarity, automatization, and other processes" (Baumeister, Gailliot, DeWall & Oaten, 2006, p. 1779).

But developing new habits is not necessarily easy. Research shows that new habits take anywhere from 18 days to 254 days to form, depending on their complexity (Lally, et al., 2009). Habits are developed from repetition, by the carving of neural pathways that connect our thoughts to our actions (James, 1892, p. 127-128). Habits can be negative, when they form a rut that prevents us from pursuing the good things in life. But habits can also be extremely positive, streamlining the way towards a happier life. Aristotle believed that happiness comes from virtue, which he defined as "being excellent at being human." With great attention and practice, one has the ability to develop good habits to become more virtuous . . . and therefore happier (Melchert, 2002,p. 189-190).

William James argued that the neural pathways, once deepened by practice and repetition, streamline our actions so that less conscious attention is required. The development of practical habits is important to how we function and grow. But habits can develop out of both negative and positive actions. The behaviors we select repeatedly are the ones that eventually become habits and have a substantial impact on our wellbeing.

James said, "we must make automatic and habitual, as early as possible, as many useful actions as we can" (p. 134). Developing these neural dispositions in a positive way allows us to accomplish great things very efficiently, while still leaving the mind free for even higher thoughts. Habits are a driver of behavior change because they automate the behaviors that lead to good (or bad) health.

People often come to a spa because they have habits that they need to change. They may realize that they are not exercising enough (or properly), not eating healthfully, not taking good enough care of themselves, or are having a hard time relaxing. Habits are powerful because they automate the process of self-control, "taking the effort out of effortful control" (Mischel & Ayduk, 2004).

Spa rituals are designed to help their guests understand and practice behaviors that will bring them greater peace and happiness. While at the spa they are able to practice meditating or sitting in silence and being mindful of the present moment. They may learn relaxation and breathing exercises or other techniques for relieving stress. They can also practice and learn new activities for physical fitness and exercise, or practice eating healthfully, perhaps with a cookbook or cooking class to bring some recipes home.

Rituals and Daily Practices

One way that spas attempt to integrate healthy activities into a person's regular life is through the concept of "daily practices." Spas, perhaps because of their roots in ancient traditions, teach us to think of daily practice not as a routine, but as a ritual. A routine becomes ritual when it is assigned greater meaning. Routines can become more meaningful via increased symbolism which communicates a deeper meaning. Commitment to a ritual is generally more emotional and often extends beyond an individual, being passed down from generation to generation (Fiese, 2007).

The idea of rituals is fading fast from our modern lifestyle and along with them our sense of identity, community and meaning (Suggs & Suggs, 2003). Who can be bothered to take extra steps if they are not necessary? Why send a handwritten letter when you can blast out a quick email from your smartphone? Why spend time preparing an intricate meal when you can pop a package into the microwave and have a complete meal in 5 minutes? These modern conveniences do help us save time, but at a certain cost. The loss of ritual comes with a loss of calmness in our pace of life and a loss of appreciation for some of the day-to-day aspects of life and living. Rituals can give some stability and purpose to our hectic, high-tech lives (Suggs & Suggs, 2003).

Ritualizing routines can also help to bring more meaning to the daily activities that people do to achieve and maintain health. Many of the behaviors that are fundamental to good health are regular routines: regular exercise, meal preparation, taking vitamins or medications, bathing, brushing, flossing, meditating, etc. Creating rituals around these activities can make them more meaningful, contribute to the emotional investment and commitment to them, and improve adherence over the long term (Fiese, 2007).

Rituals are not only about emphasizing the routine in our lives. Rituals "link an individual to moment, a community and something beyond the self" (Address, 2005, p. 224). They are important for bringing people together and also for helping people to get through transitional periods in their lives. In the religious world, for example, rituals are used to "reenact and regenerate the community's vision of the world" in times and places that are special and meaningful. Wedding ceremonies, birthdays, anniversaries, wakes and funerals, and baby showers are all examples of rituals (religious and secular) created to mark the significant transitional moments in our lives (Pargament, 1997). Birthdays, Mother's Day, Valentine's Day, anniversaries and weddings are all ritual holidays that are often celebrated in spas. The cultural rituals that we have around these special events are meant to "mark and facilitate the transition through" the most notable changes in our lives (p. 239). Spas can lend significance to the meaningful moments in people's lives by giving an outlet for people to take stock of their own wellbeing, take time for reflection, and deepen connections with the people they are close to in a very nurturing and intimate environment.

These kinds of transitional rituals become even more important as people get older. As people age, they face more and more of these prominent life transitions: "retirement, newfound freedom, empty nest, grandparenthood, moving, death of family and friends, loss of physical function. These are important markers in their lives" (Suggs & Suggs, 2003, p. 20). Rituals can help people cope with some of these facets of aging because they "make the negative situations more tolerable and meaningful and the positive situations more joyful and meaningful" (p. 20). Because we are currently experiencing a boom in longevity due to greater wealth and greater health technologies, there may be a growing demand for rituals in people's lives as the global population ages (Address, 2005).

Rituals are a prominent part of the history of any culture. Japanese baths, Chinese tea ceremonies, Hawaiian luaus, Muslim prayers, and Mexican family meals are all examples of normal activities which have taken a prominent role in their respective cultures by becoming more of a ritual than a routine. An activity becomes a ritual when its proper practice becomes more important than the time it takes to complete it. Practicing any activity in this way forces people to slow down and be present in the moment. It helps them to recognize the importance of what they are doing and to take pride in the results.

In the world of spas, these rituals might include a morning yoga stretch, daily meditation, journal writing, facial cleansing and skincare, healthful eating, brisk walks, or simply appreciating joyful moments. Spa rituals can help people to celebrate life, take care of their health, and give hope and meaning to guide them through the aging process. The activities that spa clients incorporate into their daily life can have a great effect on the goals they achieve, the happiness they experience and not only the person they are today, but the one they will become.

Beyond the Spa

I believe that a visit to a spa becomes a valuable experience when it changes how the person lives their life after they leave the spa. Only so much impact can be made during a brief spa visit. But if the spa can use positive interventions to help people change their behaviors and lifestyle in an ongoing way, they can make a substantial difference in people's lives. Within a spa setting, customers can and should practice interventions which help them to develop new habits. They should take personal responsibility for these habits and recognize the power of their own mind in creating positive outcomes. Spas are focused on treating the person holistically and interventions should engage the connections between mind, body and spirit. Interventions should build hope in spa customers and give them goal setting techniques that will help them to create positive change in their lives for long after the spa visit is over.

CHAPTER 7

Measuring a Spa's Impact on Wellbeing

I have attempted to show, through a review of the research literature from psychology, the ways that spas can enhance wellbeing, particularly across mind and spirit. Spas enhance well being by offering a break from the stresses of daily life, a chance to disconnect from technology, and an opportunity to slow down and either reflect on one's spiritual beliefs or connect with others. Spas also enhance wellbeing by teaching healthy lifestyle behaviors designed to improve health and reduce stress on an ongoing basis. But how do spas truly know they are having a positive impact on the wellbeing of their clients unless they have a system of measurement in place to detect it?

Subjective Wellbeing in the Spa

The industry clearly has appeal to consumers, but its promise to "enhance overall wellbeing" may be a lofty claim to make, unless specific data is available to show the link between spa usage and not only objective health measures, but subjective wellbeing. Subjective wellbeing measures are sometimes preferable to objective indicators since an objective measure of wellness, such as body fat percentage or resting heart rate, may be too specific to be a suitable operational definition for holistic wellbeing. Furthermore, the results of those objective measures would still require a subjective evaluative component to truly determine the "overall wellbeing" of the client (Diener, Lucas, Schimmack, & Helliwell, in press, Ch. 2, p. 4). While some research exists on the therapeutic benefits of a spa on physical health, spas should do more to determine the psychological impact of an industry that prides itself on servicing "mind, body and spirit" (Johnson & Redman, 2008).

Measuring Subjective Wellbeing

The spa industry needs a survey that can measure the impact of a spa visit on wellbeing and can highlight in greater detail which elements of the spa experience, and from which domains, the greatest benefits occur. Questions would need to be primarily subjective reports of mood, satisfaction and stress-level, but should also include some behavioral self-observations designed to help counteract potential biases in subjective measures. Since the spa industry has a focus on mind, body and spirit, the survey should ask questions that cover all three domains. For example, a survey could ask people to rate their state of wellbeing physically, mentally and emotionally. By matching up different responses to the different types of spa experiences customers have, spas could gain a greater awareness of how their services affect their guests.

Consumption of spa services continues to grow — an indication of their appeal to consumers. Spas should ask specific questions on mood and subjective wellbeing, but they should also ask their customers general questions such as, "How did you benefit from your spa experience today?" The qualitative reports of customers can help to refine these tools to become more and more specific in the future. Developing the right tool and then providing it for use in spas will help the spa industry clearly define its mission, establish its identity, and answer the question: "What's good about a spa?"

If spas were able to measure the impact of their services on the subjective wellbeing (SWB) of their clients, it would give them several advantages. First, they could test to see which treatments, services and facilities generated the greatest contribution to the wellbeing of their clients, allowing them to adjust policies, procedures, treatment menus and facility offerings for maximum benefit. They could also use the data gathered to inform hiring, training and disciplinary policies to build a team of therapists and other associates most adept at affecting SWB. And most importantly for the leaders of the spa industry, if they were able to generate and measure a positive impact on SWB they could shift public perceptions of spa services away from the idea that they are pampering indulgences and towards a belief that they are an essential part of a productive, healthful and happy lifestyle.

In "Wellbeing and Policy," Diener et al. (ch. 3, p. 2-3) said that another benefit of wellbeing measures comes from their being by nature "broad assessments" that can be used "to derive comparable values for disparate consequences." For spa managers, this kind of general indicator can give an idea of the overall impact of policies such as serving alcohol, or allowing groups in the spa. Some people will enjoy these opportunities to be more social and "let loose." But if the tranquility of the spa experience is jeopardized, it could have an adverse effect on other customers. Being able to measure the overall impact of these decisions would help spas to set appropriate policies that provide the greatest wellbeing to the majority of their customers.

Currently, spas and hotels typically ask for feedback from customers to evaluate the service provided during their stay. Questions may be asked to evaluate customers' satisfaction with the quality of the service, the attitude of the staff, and the extent and cleanliness of the facilities being offered. Once gathered, this information can be useful to help establish best practices, to create or update service standards, to create or update treatment menu offerings, for purchasing, maintenance and replacement of equipment, and for the training and/or disciplining of employees. While customers can already express their satisfaction with the service, spas should measure the actual effect on wellbeing. Possibly, this could be assessed by adding additional questions to the tool which is already being used.

Challenges of Measuring Subjective Wellbeing in the Spa Environment

Before spas can implement any kind of system of wellbeing measurement, they need to overcome several challenges. The greatest difficulties stem from the complex, multi-dimensional nature of SWB. As a construct, SWB is fairly stable and should reflect a satisfaction with life that stretches across multiple domains. It may not be realistic to think that a single visit to the spa would have an easily measurable impact on overall wellbeing, but a regular spa-goer might experience a more pronounced effect across multiple visits. The duration of one spa experience (typically 1-3 hours) may be too small to make an impact significant enough to be measurable.

It might be more effective to narrow the measurement to only those domains expected to have the greatest impact. The effect of a spa experience, for example, is not likely to have any impact on a customer's subjective feelings about his job, social life, or economic situation. But other domains, such as health, stress-level, self-esteem, and quality of leisure time might increase. A narrower focus, which excludes certain domains, and focuses on others, could be more useful and better at measuring significant impact.

It is useful to consider exactly what benefits we should expect from a spa visit. It could be argued that a spa visit has an impact on positive emotions and/or mood but not necessarily on overall wellbeing or life satisfaction. If this is the case, spas should utilize a different tool, such as the Positive And Negative Affect Scale (PANAS) or the Perception Of Mood Scale (POMS) to determine the effect of the spa visit on the emotions and/or mood. The challenge then becomes that positive mood or affect is not the only way that spas may impact overall SWB. For example a customer may come to a spa and have a painful deep-tissue massage, or an even more painful bikini waxing service that produces some negative emotions and puts her in a bad mood, but yields a result which is desirable and makes her happy in the long run.

Diener et al. (Ch. 2, p. 13-16) list several challenges with relying on affective measures as an indicator of subjective wellbeing. In a spa setting where alcohol is served for example, alcohol may influence the mood or affect of the person. And affective measures may inadvertently reflect a bias towards domains which elicit a stronger emotional response due to their evolutionary history. We have strong affective responses to foods which are high in fats and sugars for example, but subjectively we may better discriminate the mixed impact this can have on overall wellbeing (p.14). Regardless, it is only by beginning to make and evaluate some measure of these effects, that the process can be refined and over time, enhanced to get the best measurement of the holistic impact of a spa visit.

The possibility for measurement errors in this kind of data collection is another significant cause for concern. The short duration makes doing pre and post tests both cumbersome and less reliable as customers will not have sufficient time to forget their pre-test measurements and thus reduce biases. Furthermore, because they are typically paying a substantial amount for their services, cognitive dissonance theory (Festinger, 1962) predicts that they could over-report the benefits they received, in order to justify the expense. The customer would also need to feel their anonymity was protected, so they could report their state of wellbeing honestly, without concerns about who might see the data.

There is one physiological measure of wellbeing which has been getting more attention lately for its ability to serve as an indicator of psychological wellbeing. Heart rate variability (HRV) is a measure of how much variation there is in the heart rate *between beats*. This indicates the proper functioning of the autonomic nervous system responsible for the relaxation response. Higher HRV is associated with a variety of positive psychological outcomes including an ability to regulate emotions and ward off stress (Waytz, 2010). I'm predicting HRV to play an increasingly larger role in the measurement of holistic wellbeing across a variety of health domains.

A potential challenge with measuring wellbeing in the spa environment could occur when and if the research shows no, or negative impact of the spa on the clients' wellbeing, which could engender or exacerbate customer complaints and adversely affect the business of the spa. From a business standpoint, it will only be effective for the spa industry to institute this kind of measurement, if they are able to record and highlight the positive impact that spas have on SWB. If such measurements can be found across spas, then negative reports which occur on a spa by spa, or customer by customer basis could still be quite useful, especially if they correspond with customer's levels of satisfaction with their visit and likelihood to return. The management of a spa needs to know if their treatments and services are truly having the effects that are promised. When a guest has a contrary experience, they need to know what went wrong in order to correct the relationship with that customer and also to adjust their offerings accordingly to prevent such problems in the future.

Business Impact of Measuring Wellbeing

Businesses would need to have substantial preliminary information in order to feel comfortable with adopting this new kind of measurement system. For example, they would need to evaluate the risks of losing revenues from perturbed customers. There would also be costs associated with the administering of a survey or other measurement tool. These risks would have to be mitigated by the potential for increased revenues driven by the gathering of evidence that supports the importance of spa usage as a part of a healthy lifestyle.

If spas can overcome these challenges (or more likely, accept them as a part of the systematic problems with this kind of data collection,) the information could be quite useful. While I think spas are nowhere near ready to institute this as a policy across the industry, they do need to begin the foundational research to determine what areas of SWB are impacted by spas and how best to measure those impacts. Before spas can begin measuring SWB across the industry, they will need to gather baseline data and evaluate measurement tools for their effectiveness and relevance.

The spa industry defines itself as a provider of enhanced wellbeing beyond mere physical health. It is important that spas look not only at the physiological benefits of spa therapies, but the psychological impact that a spa has on the consumer. Spas seek to offer an alternative kind of healing that looks at the person holistically, and addresses their wellbeing across their mind, body and spirit. Having an accurate tool for measuring this impact could be the difference between spas existing as a mere trend or fad in our society, or revolutionizing modern medicine and what it means to be healthy in our culture.

CHAPTER 8
Conclusion

The spa industry provides a unique wellness offering in our culture. Spas deliver healing interventions in beautiful settings, touching all of the senses, and treating their clients holistically across mind, body and spirit. Consumers are drawn to spa services not only because of their healing effect, but because the experience is pleasurable. The spa is often considered a reward or a treat for the spa-goer — an experience to look forward to prior, savor during, and reminisce about afterward.

The luxurious nature of the spa experience is something that subjects spas to criticism, as if pampering has no place in the healing process and true healing can only take place within the cold, sterile halls of conventional medicine. But the popularity and appeal of spa services seems almost universal, spanning time and place in different cultures around the world and throughout history. And people are continually seeking improvements to current health care systems. There is a desire for them to be more nurturing, more holistic, more personal, and perhaps one could say, more *spa*.

Modern psychological science can help to validate the mechanisms behind some of the spas' appeal and identify where spa concepts and modalities should be integrated into other healing institutions. Through the lens of psychology, we see that the mind and spirit (thoughts, beliefs, emotions, etc.) play a powerful role in our physical health, and how we care for our physical body can also affect our psychological and emotional states. Spas do their clients a great service by looking beyond the realm of physical health. Wellness is created by increasing pleasure and positive emotions, by encouraging healthy behavior and lifestyle through education on healthy goals, habits and rituals, and by giving people a space and time for personal reflection and spiritual and emotional growth and healing. We are holistic beings and our wellness is contained as much within the whole as it is within the parts.

While spas transmit their wellness interventions through all the senses, there is an emphasis on the use of touch as a healing modality. The field of psychology teaches us that there are benefits to touch that go beyond the mere manipulation of tissues. Being nurtured and touched and having the support of other people is critical to our health and wellbeing. Ironically, one of the ways that spas help us to heal ourselves is by allowing us to be touched and cared for by another person.

Mainly, spas provide a sense of place and meaning that allows the mind to be engaged in the healing process. Psychology teaches us that the mind has a powerful role in wellbeing. Our intentions, expectations and emotions can lead us towards or away from a greater state of health. Mindfulness and relaxation are extremely important in this process because they break us out of our emotional habits that put us into a chronic state of stress. Spas emphasize reducing or relieving stress as a way to wellness, and science tells us that this may indeed be one of the best pathways to greater wellbeing.

There is an important place for the science of psychology in the world of spas. Spas can benefit greatly from studying and applying what the scientific literature yields to improve the impact they have on their clients' wellbeing. Positive psychology, in particular, with its focus on increasing optimal functioning and human flourishing, can provide insights into new and better interventions for health and happiness. Spa consumers benefit when the science of wellbeing is applied in a holistic way, helping them to reduce stress, improve health and increase their overall satisfaction with life.

This is already happening in the destination spas, according to a research study done by Mary Tabacchi, the professor who teaches the spa courses in Cornell University's School of Hotel Administration. Destination spa goers return home both healthier and happier compared to other vacationers. "They have more mental and physical energy, are more alert and agile, have greater cardiovascular fitness, a better body image and they exercise more enthusiastically than do regular vacation goers," said Tabacchi. And when they get home, "they are better able to resolve challenges and to relax."

These changes are not just at the individual level. Upon their return, these spa-goers reported that their creativity on the job was improved and they observe a "halo effect" that reaches into other areas of their lives. They say that family members observe "a definite positive change" in them and that they also felt more cared for my family, friends and colleagues (Myers, 2005).

The world needs new ways of healing that feel good, consider the whole person, and have an impact that goes beyond the individual. I think spas have the potential to change the world, but spas are not the only solution. Our science of medicine is being informed by new research, like the findings of positive psychology. All of our health institutions are evolving, but slowly. Spas benefit from a strong holistic philosophy but lack a basis in science. Medicine is all science and no philosophy. The healing institution of the future will be the one that combines a holistic approach to wellbeing with a solid grounding in scientific research. Science guides the way, but philosophy is what allows us to imagine what lies beyond the boundaries of our understanding. The secret to human wellbeing lies somewhere in the intersection of the two.

References

Acuna, L. L., & Bruner, C. (2002). El efecto de las personas sobre la salud. *Revista mexicana de psicologia,* 19(2), 115-124.

Address, R. (2005). Creating sacred scenarios. *Journal of gerontological social work,* 45(1), 223-232.

American Psychiatric Association. (2000). Diagnostic and statistical manual of mental disorders, (4th ed., text revision). Washington, DC: American Psychiatric Association.

Anderson, S., & Gantt, W. H. (1966). The effect of person on cardiac and motor responsivity to shock in dogs. *Conditional reflex,* 1(3), 181-189.

d'Angelo, R., MD (2002). Aromatherapy. In Shannon, S. (Ed.) *Handbook of Complementary and Alternative therapies in mental health.* Ch. 4, pp. 71-92.

Aristotle (1962). *Nichomachean ethics* (Martin Oswald, trans.). Indianapolis, IN: Bobbs-Merrill.

Audi, Robert, Ed. (1999). *The Cambridge dictionary of philosophy.* 2nd Edition. Cambridge, MA: University Press.

Barbieri, P. P. (1996). Confronting stress: Integrating control theory and mindfulness to cultivate our inner resources through learning mind/body health methods. *Journal of reality therapy,* 15(2), 3-13.

Baumeister, R. F., Gailliot, M., DeWall, C. N., & Oaten, M. (2006). Self-regulation and personality: How interventions increase regulatory success, and how depletion moderates the effects of traits on behavior. *Journal of Personality, 74(6)*, 1773-1801.

Ben-Shahar, T. (2007). *Happier: Learn the secrets to daily joy and lasting fulfillment.* New York: McGraw-Hill.

Blair, S. N. (2009). Physical inactivity: The biggest public health problem of the 21st century. *British journal of sports medicine, 43*, 1-2.

Bonadonna, J. R. (2002). Therapeutic touch. *Handbook of complementary and alternative therapies in mental health, 231-248.*

Bowen, S. & Marlatt, A. (2009). Surfing the urge: Brief mindfulness-based intervention for college student smokers. *Psychology of Addictive Behavior, 23(4)*, 666-671.

Boyd, C. (2007, June 4). Spas check in to local hotels, polish up personal pampering. *Orlando Sentinel (Orlando, FL).* Retrieved May 9, 2009 from http://www.accessmylibrary.com/coms2/summary_0286-30935192_ITM.

Brody, J. E. (2008, June 24). Fit, not frail: Exercise as a tonic for aging. *The New York times (New York, NY).* Retrieved May 10, 2009 from http://www.nytimes.com/2008/06/24/health/24brod.html?_r=1&scp=1&sq=%22active%20aging%22&st=cse.

Bower, J. E., Low, C. A., Moskowitz, J., Sepah, S., & Epel, E. (2009). Benefit finding and physical health: Positive psychological changes and enhanced allostasis. *Social and Personality Psychology Compas, 2,*223-244.

Brown, K. W., & Ryan, R. M. (2004). Foster healthy self-regulation from within and without: A self-determination theory perspective. In Linley, P. A., & Joseph, S., (Eds.), *Positive psychology in practice,* 105-124. Hoboken, NJ: Wiley & Sons, Inc.

Butler, J. (2007, February 1). Notable quotables from hotel industry thought leaders 2007. *Hospitality Net.* Retrieved May 9, 2009 from http://www.hospitalitynet.org/news/154000355/4030143.search?query=luxury+hotels+add+spas.

Byrne, R. (2006). *The secret.* New York: Atria Books.

Cahana, A. (2007). The placebo effect and the theory of the mind. *Pain practice, 7*(1), 1-3..

Campbell, Eileen and Brennan, J. H. (1994) Body Mind & Spirit: A dictionary of new age ideas, people, places, and terms, Rutland, Vermont: Charles E. Tuttle Company, Inc.

Centers for Disease Control and Prevention (2009). Obesity: Halting the epidemic by making health easier. *Chronic Disease Prevention and Health Promotion.* Retrieved July 28, 2009 from http://www.cdc.gov/NCCdphp/publications/AAG/obesity.htm.

Ch'i. (2009). In *Wikipedia, the free encyclopedia.* Retrieved April 12, 2009 from http://en.wikipedia.org/wiki/Ch%27i.

Charlesworth, E. A., & Nathan, R. G. (2004). *Stress management: A comprehensive guide to wellness.* New York: Ballantine Books.

Christakis, N. A., & Fowler, J. H. (2007). The spread of obesity in a large social network over 32 years. *The New England Journal of Medicine, 357,* 370-379.

Christakis, N. A., & Fowler, J. H. (2011). *Connected: The suprising power of social networks and how they shape our lives.* Back Bay Books.

Clodagh (2001). *Total design: Contemplate, cleanse, clarify, and create your personal spaces.* New York: Clarkson Potter.

Chopra, D. (2003). *The spontaneous fulfillment of desire: Harnessing the infinite power of coincidence.* New York: Crown Publishing.

Coan, J. A., Schaefer, H. S., Davidson, R. J. (2006). Lending a hand: Social regulation of the neural response to threat. *Psychological science, 17*(12), 1032-1039.

Cohen, S., & Pressman, S. (2004). The stress-buffering hypothesis. In N. Anderson (Ed.), <u>Encyclopedia of Health and Behavior</u> (pp. 780-782). Thousand Oaks, CA: Sage Publications.

Cohen, S., & Pressman, S. D. (2005). Does positive affect influence health? *Psychological bulletin, 131*(6), 925-971.

Cohen, S., & Pressman, S. D. (2006). Positive affect and health. *Current directions in psychological science, 15*(3), 122-125.

Cohen, S., Doyle, W. J., Skoner, D. P., Fireman, P., Gwaltney, J. M., Jr., & Newsom, J. T. (1995). State and trait negative affect as predictors ofobjective and subjective symptoms of respiratory viral infections. *Journal of Personality and Social Psychology, 68,* 159–169.

Cohen, S., Doyle, W. J., Turner, R. B., Alper, C. M., & Skoner, D. P. (2003). Emotional style and susceptibility to the common cold. *Psychosomatic Medicine, 65,* 652–657.

Compton, W. C. (2005). Positive psychology interventions. In *An Introduction to Positive Psychology* (pp. 182-195). Belmont, CA: Wadsworth.

Cooperrider, D. L., Whitney, D., & Stavros, J. M. (2008). *Appreciative inquiry handbook: For leaders of change.* Brunswick, OH: Crown Custom Publishing.

Crowley, C., & Lodge, H. S. (2004). *Younger next year: Live strong, fit, and sexy – until you're 80 and beyond.* New York: Workman Publishing.

Csikszentmihalyi, M. (1990). *Flow: The psychology of optimal experience.* New York: Harper & Row.

Danner, D. D., Snowdon, D. A., & Friesen, W. V. (2001). Positive emotions in early life and longevity: Findings from the nun study. *Journal of personality and social psychology, 80*(5), 804-813.

Deci, E. L., & Ryan, R. M. (1985). *Intrinsic motivation and self-determination in human behavior.* New York: Plenum.

Di Tella, R., & MacCulloch, R. (2008). Happiness adaptation to income beyond "basic needs." *National bureau of economic research, NBER working paper series, working paper 14539.*

Diener, E., & Biswas-Diener, R. (2008). *Happiness: Unlocking the mysteries of psychological wealth.* Malden, MA: Blackwell Publishing.

Diener, E., & Chan, M. Y. (2011). Happy people live longer: Subjective well-being contributes to health and longevity. *Applied Psychology: Health and Well-Being. 3*(1), 1-43.

Diener, E., Lucas, R. E., Schimmack, U., & Helliwell, J. (in press). Wellbeing and Policy.

Ditzen, B., Neumann, I. D., Bodenmann, G., von Dawans, B., Turner, R. A., Ehlert, U., & Heinrichs, M. (2007). Effects of different kinds of couple interaction on cortisol and heart rate responses to stress in women. *Psychoneuroendocrinology, 32,* 565-574.

Duckworth, A.L., Peterson, C., Matthews, M.D., & Kelly, D.R. (2007). Grit: Perseverance and passion for long-term goals. *Journal of Personality and Social Psychology, 92,* 1087-1101.

Dweck, C. S. (2006). *Mindset: The new psychology of success.* New York: Ballantine Books.

Dyer, W. W. (2004). *The power of intention.* Carlsbad, CA: Hay House.

Ellis, S. (April, 2004) Medical Spas – now visible to the consumer! *Spafinder.* Retrieved September 9, 2008, from http://www.spafinder.com/spalifestyle/insider/newsletter /medicalspas.jsp.

Ellis, S. (August 3, 2011) Spa evidence portal, www.spaevidence.com, is live! *Susie's Spa Blog.* Retrieved August 3, 2011 from http://blog.spafinder.com/spa-industry/spaevidence/.

Faulconbridge, L. F., Wadden, T. A., Berkowitz, R. I., Sarwer, D. B., Womble, L. G., Hesson, L. A., Stunkard, A. J., Fabricatore, A. N. (2009). Changes in Symptoms of Depression with Weight Loss: Results of a Randomized Trial. *Obesity.* 17(5):1009-16.

Festinger, L. (1962). Cognitive dissonance. Scientific American, 207(4), 93-107. Retrieved from http://www.csa.com.

Field, T. M. (1994). Touch hunger. In J. D. Goodman & H. C. Nusbaum (Eds.) *The development of speech perception.* The MIT Press.

Field, T. M. (1996). Touch therapies for pain management and stress reduction. *Health psychology through the life span: Practice and research opportunities,* 313-321.

Field, T. M. (1998). Massage therapy effects. *American psychologist, 53*(12), 1270-1281.

Fiese, B. (2007). Routines and rituals: Opportunities for participation in family health. *OTJR: Occupation, Participation and health 27,* 41S-49S.

Fitch, W. E. (1929). *The Carlsbad of America.* Pennsylvania: Lancaster Press, Inc.

Forman, J. (2009). Lessons from a WWII ghetto resonate with doctors today. *The Boston Globe,* (August 10, 2009).

Fredrickson, B. (2009). *Positivity: Groundbreaking research reveals how to embrace the hidden strength of positive emotions, overcome negativity, and thrive.* New York: Crown Publishers.

Freeman, D. H. (July/August 2011). The triumph of new age medicine. *The Atlantic*.

Fries, J. F., & Vickery, D. M. (2000). *Take care of yourself: The complete illustrated guide to medical self-care*. Perseus Publishing.

Gable, S. L., Reis, H. T., Impett, E., & Asher, E. R. (2004). What do you do when things go right? The intrapersonal and interpersonal benefits of sharing positive events. *Journal of personality and social psychology, 87*, 228-245.

Gantt, W. H., Newton, J. E. O., Royer, F. L., & Stephens, J. H. (1966). Effect of person. *Conditional reflex, 1*(1), 18-35.

Gattozzi, R. (1971). The effect of person on a conditioned emotional response of schizophrenic and normal subjects. *Conditional reflex, 6*(4), 181-190.

Glusac, E. (2007, July 15). The room as spa, and vice versa. *The New York times (New York, NY)*. Retrieved May 9, 2009 from http://travel.nytimes.com/2007/07/15/travel/15surfacing.html?ref=travel.

Goleman, D. J., & Schwartz, G. E. (1976). Meditation as an intervention in stress reactivity. *Journal of consulting and clinical psychology, 44*(3), 456-466.

Gollwitzer, P. M. (1999). Strong effects of simple plans. *American psychologist, 54*(7), 493-503.

Haidt, J. (2000). The positive emotion of elevation. *Prevention & Treatment, 3*(1) doi:10.1037/1522-3736.3.1.33c

Haidt, J. (2006). *The happiness hypothesis: Finding modern truth in ancient wisdom*. New York: Basic Books.

Harrington, A. (2002). "Seeing" the placebo effect: Historical legacies and present opportunities. *The science of placebo: Toward an interdisciplinary research agenda* (Guess, H. A., Kleinman, A., Kusek, J. W., & Engel, L. E. Eds.) London, England: BMJ Books.

Harvey, J. H., Pauwels, B. G., & Zickmund, S. (2002). Relationship connection: The role of minding in the enhancement of closeness. In Snyder, C. R., & Lopez, S. J. (Eds.), *Handbook of Positive Psychology* (pp. 423-433). New York: Oxford University Press.

Herron, R. E. (2011). Changes in physician costs among high-cost Transcendental Meditation practitioners compared with high-cost nonpractitioners over 5 years. *American Journal of Health Promotion (26)*1, 56-60.

Hill, N. (2007). *Think and grow rich*. Radford, Virginia: Wilder Publications.

Hinsdale, Guy A. M. (1910). *Hydrotherapy*. Philadelphia: W. B. Saunders Company.

Holmes, N. (2007). Growth versus fixed mindset diagram. Retrieved March 27, 2009 from http://www.stanfordalumni.org/news/magazine/2007/marapr/images/features/dweck/dweck_mindset.pdf.

Holt-Lunstad, J., Birmingham, W. A., & Light, K. C. (in press). The influence of a "warm touch" support enhancement intervention among married couples on ambulatory blood pressure, oxytocin, alpha amylase and cortisol. *Psychosomatic medicine*.

Hölzel, B. K., Lazar, S. W., Gard, T., Schuman-Olivier, Z., Vago, D. R., & Ott, U. (2011). How does mindfulness meditation work? Proposing mechanisms of action from a conceptual and neural perspective. *Perspectives on Psychological Science, 6,* 537-559.

Hosie, P. J., Sevastos, P. P., & Cooper, C. L. (2006). *Happy-performing managers: The impact of affective wellbeing and intrinsic job satisfaction in the workplace.* Northhampton, MA: Edward Elgar.

International Spa Association (2004). *ISPA 2004 consumer trends report: Variations and trends on the consumer spa experience.* The Hartman Group.

International Spa Association (2006a). *ISPA 2006 consumer report: Spa-goer and non-spa-goer perspectives.* Bellvue, WA: The Hartman Group, Inc.

International Spa Association (2006b). *ISPA 2006 spa-goer study: U.S. and Canadian consumer attitudes and spa use.* Bellevue, WA: The Hartman Group, Inc.

International Spa Association (2006c). *Types of spas.* Retrieved May 9, 2009 from International Spa Association Web site: http://www.experienceispa.com/spa-goers/spa-101/types-of-spas/.

International Spa Association (November, 2007) 2007 Spa Industry Study, *International Spa Association/Association Resource Centre, Inc.,* p. ii

International Spa Association (2009, April 21). *Spa: It's a lifestyle, not a luxury* [Press release]. Retrieved May 9, 2009 from http://news.prnewswire.com/DisplayReleaseContent.aspx?ACCT=ind_focus.story&STORY=/www/story/04-21-2009/0005010135&EDATE=.

Jackson, R. (1990) Waters and spas in the classical world. In Roy Porter (Ed.) *The medical history of waters and spas.* London: Wellcome Institute for the History of Medicine.

James, W. (1892). Selections from *Principles of Psychology: Briefer Course.*

Jin, P. (1992). Efficacy of tai chi, brisk walking, meditation and reading in reducing mental and emotional stress. *Journal of Psychosomatic Research,36*(4), 361-370.

Johnson, E. M., & Redman, B. M. (2008). *Spa: A comprehensive introduction.* Lansing, MI: The American Hotel & Lodging Educational Institute.

Kabat-Zinn, J. (1994). *Wherever you go there you are: Mindfulness meditation in everyday life.* New York: Hyperion.

Kahneman, D. (1999). Objective happiness. In *Wellbeing: The foundations of hedonic psychology* (ed. D. Kahneman, E. Diener & N. Schwarz), pp. 3–25. New York: Russell.

Kahneman, D. (2000). Evaluation by Moments: Past, and Future. In D. Kahneman and A. Tversky (Eds.) *Choices, Values and Frames.* (chapter 38). New York: Cambridge University Press and Russell Sage Foundation.

Kashdan, T. (2011). Naturalistic positive interventions. From a lecture at the *International Positive Psychology Association World Congress* (July).

Kaye, A. D., Kaye, A. J., Swinford, J., Baluch, A., Bawcom, B. A., Lambert, T. J., & Hoover, J. M. (2008). The effect of deep-tissue massage therapy on blood pressure and heart rate. *The journal of alternative and complementary medicine, 14*(2), 125-128.

Kendall-Reed, P., & Reed, S. (2004). *The complete doctor's stress solution: Understanding, treating and preventing stress and stress-related illnesses.* Toronto, Ontario, Canada: Robert Rose Inc.

Kidd, A. H., & Kidd, R. M. (1987). Reactions of infants and toddlers to live and toy animals. *Psychological reports, 61,* 455-464.

King, L. A. (2001). The health benefits of writing about life goals. *Personality and Social Psychology Bulletin, 27,* 798-807.

King, L. A., Eells, J. E., & Burton, C. M. (2004). The good life, broadly defined. In A. Linley, & S. Joseph, (Eds.), *Positive psychology in practice.* New Jersey: John Wiley and Sons.

Kleinman, A. Guess, H. A., & Wilentz, J. S. (2002). An overview. In *The science of placebo: Toward an interdisciplinary research agenda* (Guess, H. A., Kleinman, A., Kusek, J. W., & Engel, L. E. Eds.). London, England: BMJ Books.

Kradin, R. (2008). *The placebo response and the power of unconscious healing.* New York: Routledge.

Kutner, J. S., Smith, M. C., Corbin, L., Hemphill, L., Benton, K., Mellis, B. K., Beaty, B., Felton, S., Yamashita, T. E., Bryant, L. L., & Fairclough, D. L. (2008). Massage therapy versus simple touch to improve pain and mood in patients with advanced cancer: A randomized trial. *Annals of internal medicine, 149,* 369-379.

Lally, P., van Jaarsveld, C. H. M., Potts, H. W. W., & Wardle, J. (2009). How are habits formed: Modelling habit formation in the real world. *European Journal of Social Psychology (40)6,* 998-1009.

LaTorre, M. A. (2005). The use of reiki in psychotherapy. *Perspectives in psychiatric care, 41*(4), 184-187.

Law, L. A. F., Evans, S., Knudtson, J., Nus, S., Scholl, K., & Sluka, K. A. (2008). Massage reduces pain perception and hyperalgesia in experimental muscle pain: A randomized, controlled trial. *The journal of pain, 9*(8), 714-721.

Lewis, M. B. & Bowler, P. J. (2009). Botulinum toxin cosmetic therapy correlates with a more positive mood. *Journal of Cosmetic Dermatology, 8,* 24-26.

Linley, P. A., & Joseph, S. (2004). Applied positive psychology: A new perspective for professional practice. In P.A. Linley & S. Joseph (Eds.) *Positive psychology in practice* (pp. 3-12). Hoboken, NJ: Wiley.

Locke, E. A. (1996). Motivation through conscious goal setting, *Applied & Preventive Psychology, 5,* 117-124.

Long, A. F. (2008). The effectiveness of Shiatsu: Findings from a cross-European, prospective observational study. *The journal of alternative and complementary medicine, 14*(8), 921-930.

Low, C. A., Bower, J. E., Moskowitz, J. T., & Epel, E. S. (2011). Positive psychological states and biological processes. In K. M. Sheldon, T. B. Kashdan & M. F. Steger (Eds.) *Designing Positive Psychology: Taking stock and moving forward,* 41-50. Oxford.

Lynch, J. J. (2000). *A cry unheard: New insights into the medical consequences of loneliness.* Baltimore, MD: Bancroft Press.

Lyubomirsky, S. (2007). *The how of happiness: A scientific approach to getting the life you want.* New York: The Penguin Press.

Maddux, J. E. (2002). Self-efficacy: The power of believing you can. In Snyder, C. R., & Lopez, S. J. (Eds.), *Handbook of Positive Psychology* (pp. 277-287). New York: Oxford University Press.

Maier, S. F., & Seligman, M. E. (1976). Learned helplessness: Theory and evidence. *Journal of Experimental Psychology: General, 105*(1), 3-46. doi:10.1037/0096-3445.105.1.3

Marti, J. and Hine, A. (1995). *The alternative health and medicine encyclopedia.* New York: Gale Research Inc.

McCarthy, J. (2008, Spring). Stop fighting time: Learn how to age joyfully. *Organic spa magazine,* 42-43.

McCarthy, J. (2010). In defense of pampering. *The Psychology of Wellbeing.* (Video from New York Spa Alliance annual summit; http://psychologyofwellbeing.com/201008/video-in-defense-of-pampering.html).

Melchert, N. (2002). Aristotle: The reality of the world. The good life. In *The great conversation: A historical introduction to philosophy,* 4th ed. (pp. 186-198). Boston: McGraw-Hill.

Mischel, W. W. (1996). From good intentions to willpower. *The psychology of action: Linking cognition and motivation to behavior.* New York: Guilford Press.

Mischel, W. W. (2004). Willpower in a cognitive-affective processing system; The dynamics of delay of gratification. *Handbook of self-regulation: Research, theory, and applications,* 99-129.

Mischel, W. W., & Ayduk, O. (2004). Willpower in a cognitive-affective processing system: The dynamics of delay of gratification. *Handbook of self-regulation: Research, theory and applications,* 99-129. New York: Guilford Press.

Mischel, W., Cantor, N., & Feldman, S. (1996). Principles of self-regulation: The nature of will-power and self-control. In E. T. Higgins & A. W. Kruglanski (Eds.), *Social psychology: Handbook of basic principles* (pp. 329-360). New York: Guilford.

Moerman, D. E. (2002). Explanatory mechanisms for placebo effects: Cultural influences and the meaning response. *The science of placebo: Toward an interdisciplinary research agenda* (Guess, H. A., Kleinman, A., Kusek, J. W., & Engel, L. E. Eds.) London, England: BMJ Books.

Mogilner, C., Kamvar, S., & Aaker, J. (2011). The shifting meaning of happiness. *Social Psychological and Personality Science.*

Moliver, N., Mika, E. M., Chartrand, M. S., Burrus, S. W., Haussmann, R. E., Khalsa, S. B. (2011). Increased Hatha yoga experience predicts lower BMI and reduced medication use in women over 45. *International Journal of Yoga (4),* 77-86.

Moody, H. R. (2009). *Human Values in Aging* (Newsletter; Augus3t 1, 2009). AARP Office of Academic Affairs.

Mutrie, N., & Faulkner, G. (2004). Physical activity: Positive psychology in motion. In Linley, P. A., & Joseph, S. (Eds.), *Positive Psychology in Practice* (pp. 146-164). Hoboken, NJ: Wiley.

Myers, L. (2005). People who stay at desination spas return happier and healthier compared with other vacationers, Cornell study shows. *Cornell University News Service* (downloaded December 26, 2011 from http://www.news.cornell.edu/stories/June05/Tabacchi.spa.lm.html).

Neff, K. (2003). Self-compassion: An alternative conceptualization of a healthy attitude toward oneself. *Self and Identity,* (2), 85-101.

Newman, R. B., & Miller, R. L. (2006). *Calm healing: Methods for a new era of medicine.* Berkeley, California: North Atlantic Books.

Oaten, M. & Cheng, K. (2006). Longitudinal gains in self-regulation from regular physical exercise. *British Journal of Health Psychology, 11*(4), 717-733.

Ong, A. D. (2010). Pathways linking positive emotions and health in later life. *Current Directions in Psychological Science, 19*(6), 358-362.

Osborn, K. (May, 2006) Spa Charity Sharing from the Heart. *Massage & Bodywork.* Retrieved September 9, 2008 from http://www.massageandbodywork.com/Articles/AprilMay2006/spacharity.html.

Pargament, K. I., & Mahoney, A. (in press). Spirituality: The search for the sacred. In S. Lopez (Ed.) *Handbook of Positive Psychology.*

Peale, N. V. (1966). *The power of positive thinking.* Fawcett World Library.

Pelzez, M. W. (May 31, 2011). Plan your way to less stress, more happiness. *Time Healthland* from http://healthland.time.com/2011/05/31/study-25-of-happiness-depends-on-stress-management/.

Pert, C. (1997). *Molecules of emotion: Why you feel the way you feel.* New York: Scribener.

Pert, C. (2006). *Everything you need to know to feel good.* New York: Hay House Publishing.

Peterson, C. (2006). *A primer in positive psychology.* New York: Oxford University Press.

Peterson, C., & Seligman, M. E. P. (2004). *Character strengths and virtues: A handbook and classification.* New York: Oxford University Press.

Peterson, C., Park, N., & Seligman, M. E. P. (2005). Orientations to happiness and life satisfaction: The full life versus the empty life. *Journal of happiness studies, 6,* 25-41.

Peterson, C., Park, N., Hall, N., & Seligman, M. E. P. (in press). Zest and work. *Journal of Organizational Psychology.*

Phalen, K. F. (1998). *Integrative medicine: Achieving wellness through the best of Eastern and Western medical practices.* Boston, MA: Journey Editions.

Porter, R. (1990) Introduction. In Roy Porter (Ed.) *The medical history of waters and spas.* London: Wellcome Institute for the History of Medicine.

Price, D. D., Finniss, D. G., & Benedetti, F. (2008). A comprehensive review of the placebo effect: Recent advances and current thought. *Annual review of psychology, 59,* 565-590.

Prilleltensky, I. and Prilleltensky, O. (2006). *Promoting wellbeing: Linking personal, organizational and community change.* New Jersey: John Wiley & Sons.

Prochaska, J. O., Norcross, J. C., & DiClemente, C. C. (1994). *Changing for good: A revolutionary six-stage program for overcoming bad habits and moving your life positively forward.* New York: HarperCollins Publishers.

Prochnik, G. (2010a). *In pursuit of silence: Listening for meaning in a world of noise.* Doubleday.

Prochnik, G. (2010b). Now don't hear this. *The New York Times, May 1, 2010.* (Downloaded December 26, 2011 from http://www.nytimes.com/2010/05/02/opinion/02prochnik.html?src=tptw),

Rajagopal, S. (2006). The placebo effect. *Pschiatric bulletin, 30,* 185-188.

Rapaport, M. H., Schettler, P., & Bresee, C. (2010). A Preliminary Study of the Effects of a Single Session of Swedish Massage on Hypothalamic-Pituitary-Adrenal and Immune Function in Normal Individuals. *The Journal of Alternative and Complementary Medicine, 16*(10), 1079-1088.

Ratey, J. J., & Hagerman, E. (2008). *Spark: The revolutionary new science of exercise and the brain.* New York: Little, Brown and Company.

Reivich, K., & Shatte, A. (2002). *The resilience factor: 7 keys to finding your inner strength and overcoming life's hurdles.* New York: Broadway Books.

Rozin, P. (1999). Preadaptation and the puzzles and properties of pleasure. In D. Kahneman, E. Diener & N. Schwarz (Eds.). *Well being: The foundations of hedonic psychology.* (Pp. 3-25). New York: Russell Sage.

Rozin, P., & Royzman, E. B. (2001). Negativity bias, negativity dominance, and contagion. *Personality and Social Psychology Review, 5,* 296–320.

Rozin, P., Haidt, J., & McCauley, C. R. (1993). Disgust. In M. Lewis, & J. M. Haviland (Eds.), *Handbook of emotions.* (pp. 575-594). New York, NY, US: Guilford Press. Retrieved from http://www.csa.com.

Ryff, C. D., & Singer, B. (2002). From social structure to biology: Integrative science in pursuit of human health and wellbeing. In Snyder, C. R., & Lopez, S. J. (Eds.), *Handbook of Positive Psychology* (pp. 541-555). New York: Oxford University Press.

Sagiv, L., Roccas, S., Hazan, O. (2004). Value pathways to wellbeing: Healthy values, valued goal attainment, and environmental congruence. In: A. Linley., & J. Stephen (Eds.). Positive Psychology in practice. NJ: John Wiley.

Sapolsky, R. (2004). *Why zebras don't get ulcers.* New York: Owl Books.

Schmied, C., Waiblinger, S., Scharl, T., Leisch, F., & Bovin, X. (2007). Stroking of different body regions by a human: Effects on behavior and heart rate of dairy cows. *Applied animal and behavior science, 109,* 25-38.

Schwartz, B. (2004). *The paradox of choice: Why more is less.* New York: Ecco.

Schwartz, B., & Ward, A. (2004). Doing better but feeling worse: The paradox of choice. In P. A. Linley, & S.Joseph (Eds.), *Positive Psychology in Practice* (pp.86–104). Hoboken, N.J.: John Wiley and Sons.

Seligman, M. E. (2006). *Learned Optimism: How to Change Your Mind and Your Life.* New York: Vintage.

Seligman, M. E. P. (2002). *Authentic happiness: Using the new positive psychology to realize your potential for lasting fulfillment.* New York: Free Press.

Seligman, M.E.P. (2008). Positive health. Schwarzer, R., & Peterson, C. (Eds.). Health and wellbeing [special issue]. *Applied psychology: International review, 57,* 3-18.

Seligman, M. E. P., Steen, T. A., Park, N. & Peterson, C. (2005). Positive psychology progress: Empirical validation of interventions. *American Psychologist, 60,* 410-421.

Shannon, S., MD (2002). Introduction: The emerging paradigm. In Shannon, S. (Ed.) *Handbook of Complementary and Alternative therapies in mental health.* Ch. 1, pp. 3-20.

Shapiro, A. K., & Shapiro, E. (1997). *The powerful placebo: From ancient priest to modern physician.* Baltimore, MD: The Johns Hopkins University Press.

Shapiro, S. L., Schwartz, G. E. R., & Santerre, C. (2002). Meditation and positive psychology. In Snyder, C. R., & Lopez, S. J. (Eds.), *Handbook of Positive Psychology* (pp. 632-645). New York: Oxford University Press.

Sharma, U., & Black, P. (2001). Look good, feel better: Beauty therapy as emotional labour. *Sociology, 35*(4), 913-931.

Shusterman, R. (2006). Thinking through the body, educating for the humanities: A plea for somaesthetics. *Journal of Aesthetic Education,* 40, 1-21.

Slyomovics, S. (1993). The body in water: Women in American spa culture. In K. Young (Ed.), *Bodylore.* Knoxville, TN: The University of Tennessee Press.

Steptoe, A., Gibson, E. L., Vuononvirta, R., Williams, E. D., Hamer, M., Rycroft, J. A., Erusalimsky, J. D., & Wardle, J. (2007). The effects of tea on psychophysiological stress responsivity and post-stress recovery: A randomized double-blind trial. *Psychopharmacology, 190,* 81-89.

Streeter, C. C., , Whitfield, T. H., Owen, L., Rein, T., Yakhkind, A., Perlmutter, R. M., Prescot, A., Ciraulo, D. A., Renshaw, P. F., & Jensen, J. E. (2010). Effects of yoga versus walking on mood, anxiety, and brain GABA levels: A randomized controlled MRS study. *Journal of Alternative and Comlementary Medicine, 16*(11), 1145-1152.

Strine, T. W., Chapman, D. P., Balluz, L.S., Moriarty, D. G., & Mokdad, A. H. (2008). The associations between life satisfaction and health-related quality of life, chronic illness, and health be3haviors among U.S. community-dwelling adults. *The journal of community health, 33,* 40-50.

Suggs, P. K., & Suggs, D. L. (2003). The understanding and creation of rituals: Enhancing the life of older adults. *Journal of religious gerontology, 15*(3), 17-24.

Thaler, R. H., & Sunstein, C. R. (2008). *Nudge: Improving decisions about health, wealth, and happiness.* New Haven, CT: Yale University Press.

Trivedi, M. H., Greer, T. L., Church, T. S., Carmody, T. J., Grannemann, B. D., Galper, D. I., Dunn, A. L., Earnest, C. P., Sunderajan, P., Henley, S. S., & Blair, S. N. (2011). Exercise as an augmentation treatment for nonremitted major depressive disorder: A randomized, parallel dose comparison. *Journal of Clinical Psychiatry (72)*5, 677-684.

van Tubergen, A. and van der Linden, S. (2002). A brief history of spa therapy. *Ann Rheum Dis, 61,* 273-275.

Vaillant, G. (2002). *Aging well: Surprising guideposts to a happier life from the landmark Harvard study of adult development.* Boston, MA: Little, Brown and Company.

Vaillant, G. (2008). *Spiritual evolution: A scientific defense of faith.* New York: Broadway Books.

Valenza, J. M. (2000). *Taking the waters in Texas: Springs, spas and fountains of youth.* Austin, Texas: University of Texas Press.

Van Dam, N. T., Sheppard, S. C., Forsyth, J. P. & Earleywine, M., (2010). Self-compassion is a better predictor than mindfulness of symptom severity and quality of life in mixed anxiety and depression. *Journal of Anxiety Disorders, 25*(1), 123-130.

Walker, E. (2009, July 27). Rising obesity rates increase nation's healthcare tab. *ABC news.* Retrieved July 28, 2009 from http://abcnews.go.com/Health/WellnessNews/story?id=8185848&page=1.

Walton, Geo. E. (1874). *The mineral springs of the United States and Canada.* New York: D. Appleton and Company

Wampold, B. E., Imel, Z. E., & Minami, T. (2007). The placebo effect: "Relatively large" and "robust" enough to survive another assault.

Weiss, A. (2004). *Beginning mindfulness: Learning the way of awareness.* Novato, CA: New World Library.

Whitlock, E. P., Orleans, C. T., Pender, N., & Allan, J. (2002). Evaluating primary care behavioral counseling interventions: An evidence-based approach. *Journal of preventive medicine, 22*(4), 267-284.

Wisneski, L. A., & Anderson, L. (2005). *The scientific basis of integrative medicine.* Boca Raton, FL: CRC Press.

Wollmer, M. A. (2009). Botulinum toxin for the treatment of depression. From http://clinicaltrials.gov/ct2/show/NCT00934687.

Waytz, A. (October 5, 2010). Psychology beyond the brain. *Scientific American.* Downloaded December 23, 2011 from http://www.scientificamerican.com/article.cfm?id=the-neuroscience-of-heart.

Wong, P. T. P. (1998). Implicit theories of meaningful life and the development of the personal meaning profile. *The human quest for meaning: a handbook of psychological research and clinical applications,* (6), 311-338.

Wrzesniewki, A., Rozin, P., & Bennett, G. (2003). Working, playing, and eating: Making the most of most moments. In C. L. M. Keyes, & J. Haidt (eds.) *Flourishing: Positive psychology and the life well-lived,* 185-204. Washington, D. C.: American Psychological Association.

Yaller, R., & Yaller, R. (1974). *The health spas: A world guidebook to health spas and nature-cure centers . . . all the best places for rest and rejuvenation.* Santa Barbara, CA: Woodbridge Press.

Yancey, K. B. (2002). Spas go with the flow, into the mainstream. *USA Today.* Retrieved March 25, 2009 from http://www.usatoday.com/travel/destinations/2003-09-24-spa_x.htm.

Visit the blog . . .

The Psychology of Wellbeing
http://psychologyofwellbeing.com

About the Author

 Jeremy McCarthy has over twenty years of experience opening and operating luxury resort spas, including 14 years with Four Seasons Hotels and Resorts and 3 years opening and operating the new spa at famed La Costa Resort and Spa. Since 2006, he is the Director of Global Spa Development and Operations for Starwood Hotels and Resorts where he is responsible for the development of spas across Starwood's many hotel brands around the world.

McCarthy sat for several years on the Board of Directors for the International Spa Association and speaks regularly at spa industry events including ISPA, The Global Spa and Wellness Summit, Leading Spas of Canada, New York Spa Alliance, Washington Spa Alliance, and SPATEC. He is the author of "Become a Spa Owner," and writes regularly for *Pulse*, *LiveSpa*, *Organic Spa Magazine*, and *Positive Psychology News Daily*, as well as his own blog on holistic wellness, *The Psychology of Wellbeing* (http://psychologyofwellbeing.com.) He has a Master of Applied Positive Psychology degree from the University of Pennsylvania that he applies to his work in spas and luxury resorts and he teaches a course at University of California, Irvine on "Positive Leadership for Spas and Hospitality." When he is not working, he enjoys surfing and beach volleyball.

CPSIA information can be obtained at www.ICGtesting.com
Printed in the USA
LVOW05s1441240114

370874LV00017B/892/P